The Nursing Process and Quality Care

The Nursing Process and Quality Care

Nan Kemp
RGN, RCNT, DipN(Lond)
Nurse Adviser Quality Assurance –
Nursing Process

Eileen Richardson
RGN, SCM, RNT, MA
Principal Lecturer,
Institute of Health & Community Services,
Bournemouth University

Edward Arnold
A member of the Hodder Headline Group
LONDON   MELBOURNE   AUCKLAND

© 1994 Nan Kemp and Eileen Richardson

First published in Great Britain 1994

British Library Cataloguing in Publication Data

Available on request

ISBN 0340 581123

Whilst the advice and information in this book is believed to be true and accurate at the date of going to press, neither the authors nor the publisher can accept any legal responsibility or liability for any errors or omissions that may be made.

Typeset in 10/12 pt. Palatino by Anneset, Weston-super-Mare, Avon.
Printed and bound in Great Britain for Edward Arnold, a division of Hodder Headline PLC, 338 Euston Road, London NW1 3BH by J. W. Arrowsmith Ltd, Bristol.

Contents

Preface

Although individualised patient care and the nursing process have been with us for some time now, nurses continue to have difficulty in goal setting and as a result there is inadequate evaluation of nursing care. It was to help practising nurses in these aspects of the nursing process that we set out to write the book which was published as *Learning to Care – Effective Goal Setting*. We believe this need remains.

At this critical time of change in the NHS and in nurse education we believe there is also a need for nurses to clearly identify their role and responsibility in relation to direct patient care. Project 2000 has, and increasingly will have, effects on practice. As students spend less time contributing to service their place is being taken to a large extent by health care assistants. Clearly, the decisions about nursing must rest in the hands of the qualified nurse, including those about the tasks which should be delegated in order to ensure quality of care.

Nurses of tomorrow will have the opportunity to develop better intellectual skills, so that they may truly be 'the knowledgeable doer' (Benner, 1984). It is anticipated that the preparation for this role will have included skills of problem solving and decision making which will enhance their ability to give effective care.

Given this scenario, there is concern about the quality of patient care and for that reason we have chosen to widen the scope of the original book by adding a further section and enlarging the original work. We hope this will address this issue at the level of other steps of the nursing process. It was also felt that it would be helpful to include the changes which are taking place in the organisation of patient care as this too will affect quality.

In the second section we will first consider the present 'quality scene' in health service care. We will consider the process of setting standards and criteria and give examples of some developed by nurses in clinical practice. In the market economy in which we now operate, 'cost' has become an important issue. We have endeavoured to give some insight into the quality/cost debate as it affects nurses. The subject of auditing is one many nurses find difficult. We have reviewed the developments at present taking place in health care auditing. While describing the topic broadly, the final chapter will focus on nursing audit, the auditing of standards set and the development of quality scores.

Reference

Benner, P. (1984) *From Novice to Expert, excellence and power in clinical nursing practice, Addison-Wesley, California.*

Acknowledgements

To the four nurses who took time and trouble to critique the drafts of the manuscript, we are deeply grateful: Pam Homer, Clinical Research and Development Manager; Sarah Kemp, Staff Nurse; Liz Stevens, Director of Nursing and Quality and Rachel Withecombe, Ward Sister.

We are also grateful to the following people who so willingly answered our questions and/or freely provided information.

Luana Avalano, Denise Barnett, Sue Bowman, Libby Campbell, Ruth Campbell, Tom Catterall, Mary Critcher, Rosemary Cunliffe, Jane Edsell, Jean Frost, Clare Hale, Judith Hill, Anne Hollingworth, Sue Catteral, Caroline Wetherly, Susan Lawson, Pam Leggett, Rebecca Malby, Ann Marshall, Barbara Milburn, Marion Miles, David Moore, Christine Roberts, David Rutherford, Margaret Smith, Margaret Stewart, Tom Swan, Elaine Taylor-Wilde, Steve Wade, Sharon Waight, Karin VonDegenberg, Sheila Weeks, Janet Brown and the nurses of the Salisbury Hospitals, Terri Fox and the nurses of Ashurst Hospital.

We also acknowledge those who helped us with the original book in 1988 – Jean Heath, Gladys Law, Barry Lunt, Elaine Parker and Don Whittick.

We are also grateful to those who helped us with the typing, in particular Carol White and Christine Lingen. Their expertise and good humour saved us hours of toil and vexation.

To our families, especially Bob for getting better, and to Robert Heslop for cheering us up.

Finally to Richard Holloway, editor, for his advice and kindness and to Diane Leadbetter-Conway of Edward Arnold, who has always been courteous and helpful.

Note to the reader

For the sake of clarity the pronoun 'she' refers to a nurse and on occasions 'he' refers to a patient. No bias is intended in the use of pronouns; we trust our readers will understand. 'Patient' is used to refer to the client, resident or person receiving care.

1

Beliefs about nursing

'Nurses are in the people business' (Whittick, 1980). They are concerned with the business of caring not just in times of illness but also when people are well. Caring is surely at the very heart of nursing and is concerned not just with the tasks which nurses do but with the values which underpin those tasks. Tschudin, cited in Hinchliff *et al.* (1993), declares that 'Caring is only effective when it is rooted in a relationship which is trusting, respecting and creative. Caring is not arbitrary, but is itself guided by human values'. It is a form of loving characterised particularly by the nature of the companionship between the nurse and patient. Accepting that nurses value their business with people we must also establish the nature of nurses' beliefs about man.

Man is a unique being who lives in a society where he has family and/or friends who are significant to him. The customs and culture of that society influence his individuality as do other factors internal to him. All individuals have a variety of needs which have been classified under headings such as: physical, psychological, social and spiritual'. Needs are requirements for the maintenance of well-being'. (Wolff *et al.*, 1979).

Most of us would recognise a state of well-being in ourselves and that personal awareness is emphasised in the citation of Ledity and Pepper in Kozier and Erb (1988) where it is defined as '. . . a subjective perception of balance, harmony and vitality'.

Nursing acknowledges the individual's right to active participation in care, therefore influencing their own health state in a positive way. Perhaps for that reason there is a preference for the concept of wellness as defined by Kozier and Erb (1988): 'Wellness is an active process through which an individual becomes aware of and makes choices that lead to a more successful existence'. This active process enables the individual to reach the balance between his 'environment, internal and external' as described by Ebersole and Hess (1981) or as in the situation described by Neuman (1989) where the whole of the clients' system is in a state of balance or harmony.

There are many situations in life where needs are not being met for whatever reason and this will affect the individual and cause him problems. When this happens his state of wellness is reduced and he may turn to the nurse to help him overcome the obstacles to meeting his needs. When nursing intervention becomes necessary it does not inevitably imply that the individual's independence is reduced to any great degree.

We believe that the individual should be consulted and involved in the decisions which are made about his care and participate meaningfully in those aspects of his care which are appropriate. The patient's family and friends may also be involved in the assessment of his needs and the plan for his care, so that realistic decisions are taken which are based both on the nurse's knowledge and experience and on the patient and his family's information. In this way the patient is more likely to reach a set goal of care because he and his family know what is expected of him.

This situation of consultation and collaboration with the patient and his family is more likely to occur when there is one 'named nurse' with whom the patient can clearly identify. The standard in the Patient's Charter (DoH, 1991) that assures the patient that there should be 'a named qualified nurse, midwife, or health visitor responsible for . . . nursing or midwifery care' gives nursing the impetus to ensure this approach is fully developed in all nursing settings.

In nursing, models or conceptual frameworks are useful ways of organising one's thinking. They may certainly help to create a more informed basis for using the nursing process and therfore it may be helpful to choose a model which is appropriate for the person whose care is being planned.

A word of caution should be raised here. Nurses in this country have made use of many models which were generated in North America often in situations which were divorced from practice. They were developed and applied in a social and health culture different from our own. British nurses should stop and think very carefully before adopting them wholesale.

In this country the model described by Roper, *et al.* is based on activities of daily living. Again this may be a useful tool but it is far more desirable that nurses should critically examine their need for a model and, based on their own identified philosophy of nursing and the needs of their particular patient, think through a model for their own practice. It is likely that this will then be an eclectic model drawing on the best and most relevant work of others.

As our philosophy is embedded in the concept that man is an individual, we feel that in the organisation of care an individualised approach must be used. We see in the nursing process such an approach. As it is a systematic way of thinking about and implementing nursing care it allows for logical planning. It also allows for measurement of the effectiveness of care which is so important in these days when, as the UKCC *Code of Professional Conduct* reminds us, as a registered nurse, midwife or health visitor we are each accountable for our practice. We are expected to control our performance to ensure that the care we provide is 'the best possible within the available resources' (DHSS, 1984). If we are controlling care then it seems reasonable that we should have some measurable way of indicating that decisions we make are 'the best possible'.

Earlier we spoke of the individual turning to the nurse for help 'to overcome obstacles in meeting his needs'. His desire to do so will obviously be affected by the number and complexity of the obstacles. When we are 'in trouble 'in our everyday lives we generally look for help to our family and friends whom we trust; they know us best and we have undoubtedly already experienced and acknowledged their ability to help us 'feel better'.

Family and friends do not have nursing knowledge or skills and in the kind of situations where nursing intervention is needed, they are unable to help as they would in the everyday events of our lives. The individuals in our care do not know us, nor we them; in this situation ours is the responsibility to make the connection that will facilitate this helping process. The more skilled we are at doing this, the more effective will be our planning of care and subsequently the interventions which are carried out. The sooner, also, will the individual be able to resume the active process of creating harmony and balance in his life.

This relationship between effective care and personal contact is illustrated in the following diagram from Whittick (1980).

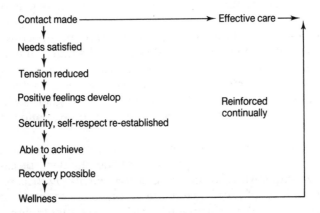

Fig. 1.1 The Wellness Cycle – the effect of a sound relationship on the sick.

This cycle indicates the security that such a relationship can bring and the reinforcement which makes recovery possible. Once the client is switched into a sound relationship with the carer, wellness can be achieved. This relationship is dependent on the nurse being able not only to identify needs but also to develop awareness of the crucial nature of feelings.

The ability to communicate accurately is important not just between the nurse and the patient but also between the nurse, the patient's family and those significant to him. Families and friends are usually part of the patient's support system and therefore their contribution must be taken into account. Those who are of significance to the patient can only participate appropriately in his care if they are involved in the decision making. Experience shows that in psychiatry, for example, the patient's problems are sometimes seen to be rooted within the family, so that involving them from the beginning is not just a bonus but a necessity.

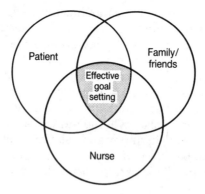

Fig. 1.2   Good communication is necessary for effective goal setting.

At the assessment interview and in the planning phase we are concerned to identify the problems and needs of the individual in our care. When this has been done we need to set against each problem the goal or anticipated outcome which our care is expected to achieve. This is often an area of weakness in the planning cycle. If goals are not clearly set we may have difficulty in correctly evaluating the patient's progress and our practice.

Not only should goals be clearly set but they should be written in such a way that there is a clear indication of the standard of care we are seeking. A standard, according to *Chambers English Dictionary* (1988), is 'the definite level of excellence required' or, to quote the *Concise Oxford Dictionary* (1992), 'the principle to which others should conform – the degree of excellence required for a particular purpose'.

The patient deserves no less than the best and all the experience and knowledge of the qualified nurse should be in evidence in these important decisions. When put into practice these decisions should be regularly and conscientiously evaluated so that their effectiveness can be measured and the patient's progress thus monitored.

This book is about good practice. Before we can act we have to clearly think out our beliefs about nursing. Before we can put our beliefs into practice we have to have in place a framework which will make this possible. In the next chapter we discuss methods of organising the delivery of care.

References

Chambers English Dictionary (1988) MacDonald, A.M. (ed.). W.R. Chambers, Edinburgh.

The Concise Oxford Dictionary (1992) Allen, R.E. (ed.). Oxford University Press, London.

Department of Health (1991) *The Patient's Charter*. HMSO, London.

Department of Health and Social Security (1984) *Health Service Management. Implementation of the NHS Management Inquiry Report*. HC (84)13, HMSO, London.

Ebersole, P. and Hess, P. (1981) *Towards Healthy Ageing*. C.V. Mosby, London.

Hinchliff, S.,Schober, J. and Norman, S. (eds) (1993) *Nursing Practice and Health Care*, 2nd edn. Edward Arnold, London.

Kozier, B. and Erb, G (1988). *Concepts and Issues in Nursing Practice*. Addison-Wesley, California.

Neuman, B. (1989) *The Neuman Systems Model*. Appleton and Lange, California.

United Kingdom Central Council (1992) *Code of Professional Conduct*, 3rd edn. UKCC, London.

Whittick, D. (1980) *Nurse Education and Rheumatology*. Paper presented at the Rheumatology Conference, Harrogate.

Wolff, L., Weitzel, M., Fuerst E.V. *et al.* (1979) *Fundamentals of Nursing*. J.B. Lippincott, Philadelphia.

2

The organisation of patient care

If we really believe that individualised care is a means of providing a quality service, then we have to choose a method of organising nursing work that makes individualised care a reality. In this chapter we intend to discuss some of the systems in use for organising patient care and to make some general suggestions on how to implement a patient care system that puts the needs of patients first.

Critical to the implementation of any new system of organising nursing work is the necessity to consider the place of accountability, responsibility, autonomy and advocacy.

> **Accountability** is: an integral part of professional practice since in the course of that practice, the practitioner has to make judgements in a variety of circumstances and be answerable for those judgements . . . The practitioner is subject to the Code (*the Code of Professional Conduct*) and has an accountability for her actions or omissions.
>
> (UKCC, 1989)

Accountability means 'bound to give account, responsible (for things, to persons)' and **responsibility** can mean 'morally accountable for actions, capable of rational conduct' (*Concise Oxford Dictionary* 1982). On a simple level professional accountability is being answerable for the work one does and being able to give reasonable argument and to take the necessary consequences. However, the nurse should not be held accountable unless she has been given the authority to be so. Equally no one should be accountable unless they can do the work and understand and accept the responsibility. Role specifications or job descriptions itemise the requirements of the role but some requirements may not be clearly stated. All nurses should be cognisant of the *Code of Professional Conduct* (UKCC, 1992) which goes some way to clarifying the position of the nurse.

Autonomy is a term much used today – it means 'personal freedom, freedom of the will' (*Concise Oxford Dictionary*, 1982) or the power or right of self government (*Chambers Dictionary*, 1980). In the context of organising patient care this means the nurse has the freedom to make decisions based on her knowledge and her experience without necessarily having to consult other professionals. However, this can be a difficult position to be in for someone who is unsure of themselves. It is also dangerous for those who are overconfident. The subject of autonomy has to be addressed and managers have to take action to ensure the nurse is qualified, competent and understands her role in accepting this responsibility.

'**Advocacy** is concerned with promoting and safeguarding the well being and interests of patients and clients.' (UKCC 1989). It is presumed by many nurses that the qualified nurse can take on the role of advocate with ease. This is not so – it is not a simple undertaking. It is only simple if the patient's wishes are clearly understood, and relatives and/or other disciplines are prepared to listen. Some groups of health carers view advocacy as a distinct activity and nurses working in such groups are not necessarily recognised as the natural advocate; the role may be taken by another member of the multidisciplinary team. But it seems to us that the nurse who has accountability for the care of the patient should also accept that she is bound to protect the rights of patients, particularly if they are unable to do this for themselves. As Cabell (1992) says, 'Advocacy remains an integral part of good nursing and is a role that should be valued and carefully considered'. Advocacy is a complex subject and must be acknowledged as such.

The named nurse

In Chapter 1 we referred to the Patient's Charter and the concept of the named nurse; we now focus on that concept in more detail. The Royal College of Nursing in 1992 stated:

> In the context of the Patient's Charter and the 'named nurse' initiative there is renewed debate about the 'best' way to care for patients. The RCN believes that although there are some systems that are more conducive to the therapeutic values of nursing, there is no one 'right' way of organising nursing care delivery for all settings . . . It is for each nursing team to choose the system that best matches the needs of the patient in their care.

This seems wise advice. We must also be careful not to 'go overboard' on one system just because it is fashionable or it looks easier than others.

Christine Hancock, General Secretary to the RCN, writing to all members about the named nurse (Hancock, 1992a), points out, 'The RCN believes that a named nurse can be a nurse on any part of the register who is giving direct care and is properly prepared and supported in her role'. Wright (1992), in answering some of the concerns nurses may be having about the named nurse, points out that:

The organisation of care under this system is designed to promote maximum continuity and coordination throughout the patient's stay. Whenever possible the same nurse should care for the same patient . . . it may involve supervising others in the delivery of that care or handing care over to another nurse when the named nurse is going to be absent.

Christine Hancock (1992b), in commenting on the Patient's Charter, says:

There is a need for creative thinking and planning by all concerned. It will be necessary to review skills mix . . . to ensure that sufficient qualified nurses are available to take the concept forward into practice.

In some areas the staffing implications will require a reassessment of the management stop-gap measures whereby nurses are moved to different work areas and those nurses who plan their rotas of staff well will cease to have to support those who do not. An advantage may be that some managers who are not nurses will have to become more aware of what nurses actually do. This is important and could enhance their role and credibility and help their staff. The way care is organised should reflect the needs of patients and the beliefs of nurses and the commitment of the unit or trust to give a quality service.

There are many ways of organising care; we will discuss the following:

1. Primary nursing
2. Team nursing
3. Patient allocation
4. Key worker
5. Case management.

Primary nursing

Maria Manthey (1973a), the developer of primary nursing, defined it as 'The delivery of comprehensive, continuous, coordinated and individualised patient care through a primary nurse who has autonomy, accountability and authority to act as chief nurse for her patients'. In 1988 she also said: At its best primary nursing is simply a way of organising people on the staff and the work to be done in a common sense system based on professional organisational principles cited by Black (1992).

In 1992 the RCN described primary nursing as 'a professional model of practice, in which a qualified nurse is responsible and accountable for the nursing care of a case load of patients for the entire duration of their care in a particular setting' and 'the values underpinning primary nursing centre on the belief that the nurse–patient relationship is therapeutic. It provides an environment and philosophy in which nurses can achieve their maximum potential in patient centred care'. When the primary nurse is not on duty the patient is looked after by an associate nurse – both are qualified nurses. Ideally, untrained members of the nursing team will also be allocated to work with the same primary nurse, thus enhancing continuity of care.

The primary nurse has to a large extent autonomy of action as it relates to patient care. She does, however, remain accountable to the ward sister or senior nurse for the standard of her practice. She may on occasions act as an associate nurse for another primary nurse. She will also facilitate the professional development of the associate nurse. The primary nurse and the associate nurse act as mentors to student nurses.

Primary nurses are involved with caring for a group of patients. However, there is also a managerial role, carried out by the ward sister, which is essential for primary nursing to work effectively. Some directly managed units or NHS trusts have changed the title of the ward sister to, for example, senior clinical nurse, senior ward nurse, ward coordinator, ward manager or consultant nurse.

The ward sister has an enabling, coordinating, monitoring and supporting role and she is also a counsellor. It is she who guides the effective implementation of primary nursing. She continues to manage resources, which for some may include budgeting and she also maintains an effective learning environment. Her role includes being involved in appointing new nursing staff. It is she who assigns the primary nurses to patients. Kemp (1983) reported how at one medical centre in America an annual peer review was carried out, whereby the primary nurses evaluated each other's practice. The unit leader (ward sister) discussed the findings with the nurses whose work was being reviewed. The results were on occasion used to justify promotion. Similarly an effective ward sister could involve a primary nurse in the assessment of an associate nurse for promotion. A problem some ward sisters experience is accepting the right of the primary nurse to make decisions without necessarily consulting them. However, the ward sister is still responsible for the standards of care; she 'monitors and assesses the nurses' work and assists them to overcome any deficiencies' (Hunt 1988). The ward sister herself needs support from her manager because primary nursing does mean a big change in her role and she may feel she is losing contact with patient care. She may also feel she has lost status as far as her paramedical colleagues are concerned. The ward sister is expected to help the nursing staff cope with their new roles, but does not necessarily have anyone to help her with her changing role. The manager should support her and the primary nurses should also be sympathetic to the sister's need to adjust to the new system.

The ward sister may on occasions act as a primary nurse, but given the demands of her role it is easier if she acts as an associate nurse when one is needed. However, if she were able to act as a primary nurse to one or two patients, she could act as a role model to her primary nurses and it would also enable her to understand their role and give her credibility. The ward sister does need to have an awareness of current changes in health care practices and policies to enable her to carry out her role effectively.

A misinterpretation about primary nursing is that the primary nurse is on call for 24 hours. This is not so; if it were, there could be problems with pay and grading, not to mention nurses not having a rest from work. The primary nurse prescribes the nursing care for the 24 hours but in her absence, she hands over the care to an associate nurse, who may change the prescription of care if it is necessary. The patients are told when the primary nurse is going off duty and who is taking over from her. When a patient is readmitted he can, if he wishes, be given the same primary nurse, always supposing the nurse does not have too heavy a case load of patients.

A breakdown in relationship between the primary nurse and the patient can occur with neither one able to relate effectively with the other. It is a situation that has to be accepted and dealt with promptly in a professional manner. 'Reassignment should be handled quickly, with a minimum of fuss and without permitting the event to become an issue' (Manthey 1988). Nonetheless, the reason for any breakdown in relationship between the patient and nurse should be explored with the primary nurse. The ward sister should quietly monitor the situation in an attempt to prevent any further repercussions. The complexity of the patient–nurse partnership is referred to by Black (1992) who states, 'Partnership between the primary nurse and a patient should be based on trust and that will not exist unless control within the relationship is shared . . . Partnership is a complex phenomenon'. She further stresses that primary nurses wishing to be partners in care require educational preparation and support.

Medical and paramedical staff may find difficulty in having to communicate with a variety of staff whereas in the past they have talked to the nurse in charge of the ward. The UKCC (1992) in clause 6 of the *Code of Professional Conduct*, directs all nurses, midwives and health visitors as follows:

'As a registered nurse, midwife and health visitor, you are accountable for your practice and, in the exercise of your professional accountability, must: work in a collaborative and cooperative manner with health professionals and others involved in providing care and recognise and respect their particular contribution within the care team.

Before introducing primary nursing, involve all the appropriate disciplines. Make sure there is some way of recognising the patient's primary nurse. Have a small noticeboard above the patient's bed with the name of the nurses caring for the patient on it. Have a noticeboard in some central area, where other care staff can see it, to give up-to-date information about which primary nurses is assigned to which patient. Consider having photographs of the nurses displayed so they are easily recognised by patients, staff and visitors.

The implementation of primary nursing on night duty can be difficult, although internal rotation can overcome some of the problems. Permanent night staff can act as associate nurses but they must be given the same preparation as day staff and the same access to literature and educational resources. It is difficult to see how a permanent night nurse can act as a primary nurse, because she does not have the same opportunity to relate to the patient's relatives or friends or to other professional involved in his care. Most patients should be asleep for a significant part of her span of duty .The fact that she cannot be a primary nurse may be disheartening for the highly skilled person, who works permanent night duty. We do see the advantages of permanent night staff acting as associate nurses.This would ensure continuity of care and also encourage good relationships between day and night staff, because there would be more encouragement for them to meet to discuss care and to get to know each other. The night sister or night manager can take on a coordinating and advisory role to associate nurses or primary nurses on internal rotation.

How individual nurses interpret and implement primary nursing can vary; it will depend in part on the environment in which they work, together with the motivation of the ward sister and manager. The skills mix of the nursing team will influence the effective implementation of primary nursing, particularly when the nurses are new to their role. The system calls for sufficient qualified nurses of the right grade to be primary nurses; this has cost implications which some managers may not be able to meet. There is no universal formula as to the number of patients each primary nurse should care for. The allocation of patients depends on many factors including the patient's need for nursing care, the input from other professionals, the ability and experience of the primary nurse. The values underlying the care the nurses give or wish to give will also influence how nurses interpret and implement primary nursing. As we indicated in our first chapter, we believe that for nursing to be effective, it has to be based on a philosophy about the rights of individuals to be consulted and to make decisions about their care when able to do so. Without a commitment to the rights of patients, primary nursing cannot be implemented effectively.

There is now a great deal of literature on the subject of primary nursing. The King's Fund Centre Foundation of Nursing Studies have produced an introductory guide to primary nursing edited by Francis Black (1992) which makes useful reading for those people who are already practising primary nursing or intending to implement it in the future.

The King's Fund established a national primary nursing network and some regional health authorities have set up regional networks to support primary nursing.

In this chapter we plan to list the advantages and disadvantages of the systems we are discussing. Those relating to primary nursing are as follows:

Advantages:

- Individualised care is a reality.
- The patient is more likely to be involved in the planning of his care.
- The named nurse concept is a reality.
- There is continuity of care.
- The patient knows the nurses who care for him and this should give him a feeling of security and trust in them.
- There are improved communications between the patient, the family and the nurse.
- The patient receives total care from the same two or three nurses.
- The patient has an advocate if he needs one.
- The patient's care is recorded and reported by nurses who know about his care in detail.
- Discharge planning is effective.
- The primary nurse acts as a role model to the associate nurse.
- It provides increased professional development of the primary nurse and associate nurse.
- The ward sister is the clinical nurse adviser.
- The ward sister is able to develop her managerial and professional skills.
- It enhances interdisciplinary partnership because the primary nurse has greater knowledge about individual patients.

Disadvantages

- The primary nurse can be overwhelmed by the responsibility, if not fully prepared and not specifically appointed for the post and not given support.
- Some primary nurses can become overconfident and fail to seek advice.
- A primary nurse may become autocratic.
- There is a risk of the primary nurse being over-protective.

- 'The primary nurse may become over-involved or over-identify with one of her patients and this may lead to open disagreement about care strategies between primary nurses, causing division in the nursing team' (Bowers, 1989).
- Permanent night nurses cannot be primary nurses.
- Night nurse managers or night sisters may not have a specific role in the primary nurse project.
- The ward sister may cease to communicate with patients.
- Paramedical and medical staff have to communicate with a number of different nurses to obtain information about the patients to which they have to give therapy or who are under their care, which they may see as time wasting.

Team nursing

A popular method of organising care which is:

> . . . based on the belief that a small group of nurses working together led by one nurse can give better care than if they work individually. It uses the skills of all team members so that the client gets the best care available. This small team is responsible and accountable for their group of patients during the whole of the patient's hospital stay.
>
> (RCN, 1992)

From a nurse management point of view team nursing can be seen to be an effective way of deploying the qualified nurses who are available.

The ward sister decides the composition of the teams and allocates the patients to a group, according to the admitting doctor or on a geographical basis – the ward being divided into sections. Sometimes the allocation is influenced by a fair division of the number of patients according to their dependency categorisation. The ward sister receives a daily report on each patient's progress and supervises when required. At times she may take over a team leader role. The role of the ward sister may not change very much with the implementation of team nursing.

The team leader is a first level nurse who is responsible and accountable to the ward sister for the care given to the group of patients. She should have leadership and some management skills; this means, amongst other things, capitalising on the particular skills of individual nurses in the team. She should at the same time ensure unqualified nursing staff are supervised and given learning opportunities. There is a need for effective communication between team members and with the person in charge of the ward.

There are a variety of ways in which team nursing is interpreted. For example:

1. All the team members work together to give care to their group of patients; no one member is specifically allocated to any particular patient.
2. Nurses are allocated, by the leader, to care for the same patients for a number of days. Team members help each other as required and progress of care is communicated to everyone in that nurse team. The team leader supervises, helps and guides the team members.
3. A modified form of primary nursing, whereby qualified nurses are allocated to care for patients for the length of the patient's stay. The individual team nurse has more autonomy of action, she assesses the patient's needs, prescribes care and evaluates the care, but she is answerable to the team leader. The team leader also cares for a small number of patients. The team members continue to support each other.

Usually in team nursing the unqualified nursing staff are allocated by the team leader according to need. The student nurses work with their mentors.

In long stay areas, nurses may be allocated to care for patients for a fixed span of time, perhaps for two months. The advantages can be: nurses get to know different patients more closely; the patients benefit from a different team, because there is the stimulus of making new relationships and having someone take a fresh look at their nursing care problems. However some patients may not understand or like this change and therefore a clear explanation of the reason for the change should be provided.

Some groups of night nurses do practise team nursing with the most senior nurse on duty acting as team leader and the other nurses being responsible for the care of particular patients during their span of night duty. But we have to acknowledge that this is often impractical due to the small numbers of staff.

There may be some difficulty in implementing the named nurse concept with the team approach, whereby any member of the team gives the care to a patient. However, the team leader could be identified as the named nurse.

Advantages

- Continuity of care is practised.
- The patient knows the nurses who care for him, which should ideally enhance his security and trust in the staff.
- Communications between relatives and nurses are enhanced.
- The patient's care and progress are reported on by nurses who know about the patient.

- There is always someone available who knows about the patient.
- All grades of staff are given a role within the team.
- There is team support for staff.
- All the special skills of the team members can be used.
- It is a safe learning environment for the least experienced nurse.
- The team leader acts as a role model for the less experienced nurses.
- The team leader's role, responsibility and learning potential is increased.
- Communications between team members are enhanced.
- Some of the ward sister's previous responsibilities may be allocated to the team leader, leaving the ward sister more time to extend her teaching and managerial role.

Disadvantages

- Task allocation may occur within the team.
- There may be a tendency for team members to become dependent on the team leader and not develop professionally.
- There may be unhealthy competition between teams.
- The ward sister may experience difficulty in allowing the team leader to lead.
- Medical and paramedical staff may experience problems in knowing which nurse to approach to discuss the patient's care.
- The named nurse concept may not be fully implemented.

Patient allocation

A term with more than one meaning; it can refer to a whole gamut of ways of organising patient care. However, today it is more likely to mean a nurse being allocated to care for one or more patients for her span of duty. She is not necessarily allocated to the same patient on the following days.

The way patient allocation works is often dependent on the philosophy of the ward sister and the resources available. The allocated nurse may be expected to follow routine procedures, referring to senior staff when changes are required. She may, however, be given freedom to organise and give care according to the individual needs of the patient at the time. Nurses working in this system often express frustration because they are not able to care for the patient for any length of time, and the people working with them are not constant either.

Advantages

- Patients receive total care – but usually from a different nurse every shift.
- Nurses get to know a variety of patients.
- The ward sister assigns patients with different dependency levels according to the ability of the individual nurses.

Disadvantages

- Continuity of care is not guaranteed.
- Planned care may not be based on a full understanding or knowledge of the patient's individual nursing needs.
- Untrained staff may not have a specific role.
- The named nurse concept may not be implemented.
- There may not be job satisfaction for the allocated nurse.
- The allocated nurse may feel frustrated because she has no continuity of practice.

Key workers

Key workers usually function as members of a multidisciplinary team.

> Key workers operate similarly to primary nurses, but may be any member of the multidisciplinary team. The team decides which member will be the most appropriate person to coordinate care for the individual client. Where the patient's dominant need is for nursing care, the key worker would normally be a nurse.
>
> (RCN, 1992)

This system can be seen in many units looking after people with learning difficulties and in some mental health units, or in any other unit where a multidisciplinary team approach to care is used. The philosophy underpinning this system is that all members have something to contribute but it is the key worker who coordinates the care. The multidisciplinary team members meet at intervals to evaluate the client's progress, suggest any changes in therapy or care and to support each other.

The role of the ward sister is similar to that in primary nursing but in addition she may take on some special task as her contribution to the team effort; for example she may teach or lead the patient's social activities. She may also act as a key worker to a small number of patients. The named nurse concept can be implemented when the key worker is a nurse.

Advantages

- The patient's progress and future are considered from more than one perspective.
- Co-ordinated care is assured.
- Individualised care is a reality.
- Continuity of care is assured.
- The patient knows who his key worker is.
- The key worker is the patient's advocate.
- There is always someone available who knows about the patient.
- Communications with relatives and guardians are enhanced.
- Good communication between the caring disciplines and outside agencies should be effective.
- The patient benefits from a team of varying specialists.
- The professional development of the key worker is supported.
- Safe learning environment for the least experienced person.
- The team act as a support system for each other.
- The named nurse concept is a reality for those patients who have a nurse as their key worker.

Disadvantages

- The key worker concept may engender professional rivalry.
- The patient may be put in a dependent position.
- The manager of the unit/ward may take on too much work.
- Some members may have difficulty working in a democratic team.
- The key worker may become too involved with the patients.
- Permanent night staff cannot be key workers.

Case management

Case management has become more widely known since the publication of the White Paper *'Caring for People'* (DoH, 1989), with its pledge to make proper assessment and good case management the cornerstone of high quality care. The RCN (1992) explains:

> Case management can be seen as an extension of the principles of primary nursing. However, the environment is less restricted. The nurse manages the patient's care as their primary nurse from the patient's first contact with the service (e.g. outpatients, visits to the GP, hospital stay) until their discharge from the service. The case manager may also have responsibility for the management of resources including staffing.

The concept of case management has many interpretations, but it is a system that can be used for most patient groups, although at present it would seem to be most used where: community and hospital services combine, in psychiatry and for people with learning difficulties. We feel this system could be introduced to units which have nursing beds, where patients are admitted primarily for nursing care. The nurse in such areas already has the right to admit, discharge and refer the patient to other agencies. District nurses who continue to care for patients when they are admitted to hospital can act as case managers. However case management is not the preserve of any one professional group; for instance, many social workers have used the approach in support of their clients.

In nursing case management the nurse extends her primary nurse or key worker role. Her normal role of coordinating the patient's care is enlarged to include all aspects of his care, which includes the effective use of resources and services available to him. She works closely with other health professionals to develop collaborative care plans, generally known as case management plans (CMP). She evaluates the effectiveness of that care often with such tools as critical paths or care maps. 'The critical path is an abbreviated one page version of the processes required by the CMP which shows the critical or key events that must occur in a predictable and timely order (Zander, 1988). The case manager monitors the patient's progress through the critical path, records variations from the path and makes alterations in collaboration with other health care professionals.

The Research and Development for Psychiatry (RDP) are overseeing a three year project on case management. This was established in 1989 with a combination of funding from the Department of Health, regional and district health authorities, social service department and the Gatsby Charitable Trust. 'Case managers have been recruited from psychiatric nursing social work, occupational therapy, psychology and non-professional backgrounds' (Ford & Ryan, 1992). The project set up pilot schemes to improve the community care of those with long term mental illness. Lear *et al.* (1991), describing a pilot scheme in this project, writes:

> Case management is a client-centred system of care which ensures that a named person, the case manager, works alongside the client. The client's various needs are met in a coordinated, effective and efficient manner. Case managers act as needs assessors and gatekeepers to other community services . . . they also deliver basic hands-on therapeutic care. Personnel from other agencies are coopted into the care package when their expertise is required and work alongside the client and case manager as specialist care deliverers or advisers.

The research programme will gauge the impact of case management on the client and all those involved in the project. A computerised monitoring system has been developed so that the data can be used for planning purposes. Lear and her co- writers end by saying, 'Through following this approach we believe we have taken a positive step towards implementing genuine community care'.

Similarly:

> In the nursing development unit at the Royal Victoria Infirmary, Newcastle upon Tyne, a study to introduce and evaluate nursing case management is currently underway. The study focuses on elderly patients with fractured neck of femur and will look at the process of introducing a system of case management and the outcomes for patients and the service as well as a range of costs. Considerable work has already been undertaken to develop multidisciplinary critical pathways,and to design the most appropriate model to suit local circumstances, educate the staff and collect the baseline data which will be used for the subsequent evaluation.
>
> (Hale, 1993)

Bergen (1992) reviewed case management and its relevance to community care. Her paper is helpful to people wanting to know more about the theoretical frameworks, definitions and research projects. She succinctly identified the issues managers should consider when examining case management. Whilst focusing on community nursing care, Bergen makes an observation which should apply to all new systems where vulnerable people are involved and resources are scarce:

> The opportunity is to consolidate those traditional practices which remain both relevant and essential; the challenge is to engage in new ways of working collaboratively in order to coordinate care more effectively . . . further descriptive and evaluative work in the area is called for.

On the surface the concept of case management would seem to meet the new Health Service purchaser/provider culture; that health carers must give a quality and cost effective service. But it will only be credible if it keeps the clients' and the staff's well being as the central focus and if the concept is clearly understood. It will take a big investment of time and money to educate nurses to carry out their new role particularly as it relates to planning for the effective use of resources and evaluating how effectively they have been used. The logistics of being responsible for patients throughout their illness episode is something that will also have to be addressed. Nurses should not be expected to undertake two roles concurrently. All case managers should be given effective support, including education and the opportunity to discuss their new role. However, it is reassuring to health professionals and social services that case management is now being researched by a number of centres for too often in the past systems were implemented without any knowledge of their validity.

Advantages

- It is possible to take a wider view of the patient's needs and to plan holistic care with the patient.
- The patient is involved in planning his care.
- The patient's progress and future are considered from more than one perspective.
- Coordinated performance by all involved agencies is assured.
- Coordinated and individualised care is a reality.
- Continuity of care is assured.
- Collaborative care is planned and evaluated systematically.
- The patient knows who his case manager is.
- The patient has an advocate.
- Communication with relatives or guardians is enhanced.
- There is a flexible approach to care.
- Nurses become purchasers on behalf of or with the patient.
- The case manager develops an understanding of resource management and uses that knowledge for the benefit of the patient and the community.
- Duplication of effort on behalf of patients by professional groups ceases.
- Interpersonal relationships between disciplines are improved. The case manager is able to develop managerial skills.
- Resources are used effectively and fairly.
- Communication between the caring disciplines and outside agencies should improve.
- Achievement of client outcomes within a fiscally responsible time frame is enhanced.
- Resources of the hospital (and community) are utilised more efficiently.
- Timely discharge of patients is facilitated (Iyer *et al.*, 1991).
- The named nurse concept is a reality for those patients who have a nurse as their case manager.

Disadvantages

- Cost containment may be given priority over care and planning.
- The case manager may have too heavy a case load.
- Some case managers may have difficulty working closely with agencies who are not health professionals.
- The case manager may take on a paternalistic role.
- Some members of the health team who have responsibility for the patient may refuse to be involved in case management.

- The variations in interpretations of case management may lead to a reactionary approach from staff.
- The patient's needs may not be fully met whilst the case manager learns her new role.
- Long term care relationship between patient and case manager may prevent a fresh approach being taken.
- May be psychologically stressful for staff.
- Case management requires a great deal of planning and cooperation to establish the system.
- It may be difficult to obtain the cooperation of physicians in defining how to manage certain case types (Iyer *et al.*, 1991).

Getting started

The ward sister or nurse manager, when choosing a new system for organising nursing care, has to be aware of the implications of change, how it is going to affect roles and resource allocation. Whatever system of patient nursing care is chosen, there is a real need to have discussions before any changes are made. The environment needs to be right and no one system should be accepted until it is considered feasible for the patients, the staff and the community.

There may also be a need to budget for a change in nursing staff grades and mix. New job descriptions may need to be written. There is a real need to anticipate and plan the effects of change, not only from a monetary point of view but for the effect it may have on staff who will need positive support.

We suggest the following will aid a smooth implementation of a new system:

- Read around the subject.
- Consider the effects of change and be prepared for negative responses.
- Consult and discuss the favoured system, involve all grades of ward staff, include medical and paramedical personnel, allow people to voice their concerns.
- Identify a facilitator and provide her or him with any necessary education.
- Devise an action plan with short and long term objectives.
- Involve the manager and find out what resources are available.
- Negotiate for money to pay for education, supplies, visits and speakers.
- Visit sites known to be successfully using the system and prepare a list of questions to ask the 'successful people'.

Having reached a conclusion as to the most effective system available:

- Inform staff, including medical and paramedical staff and answer their concerns.
- Provide education on the effects of change and the theory of the system and experiential workshops to practise any new activity, such as bedside handover.
- Identify skills required and the scope of each role; ensure everyone knows everyone else's role.
- Write guidelines on how to use the new system.
- Set up a pilot project.
- Devise a monitoring system to gauge opinions about the project from staff, patients and relatives; this too may have budgetary implications.
- Join any support groups such as a regional or local district network and if there aren't any, set one up.
- Advertise the project to inform patients and visitors what the project is about.
- Have a board where colleagues, patients and visitors to the ward can easily identify the nurse with responsibility for a particular patient.

The manager and/or ward sister should be available to support staff. If the system does not work after the pilot project has ended, explore why and if it is not appropriate for the ward or team and cannot be altered, choose another system or return to the previous one.

It can be seen that there are many interpretations of the different systems for organising nursing care but what is important is that patients receive good continuous and coordinated care by a named nurse who is responsible for patient care and well prepared for the role and who works effectively to give good quality care.

References

Bergen, A. (1992) Case management in community care: concepts, practices and implications for nursing. *Journal of Advanced Nursing*, **17**, 1106–13.

Black, F. (ed.) (1992) *Primary Nursing. An Introductory Guide*. King's Fund Centre, London.

Bowers, L. (1989) The significance of primary nursing. *Journal of Advanced Nursing*. **14**, 13–19.

Cabell, C. (1992) The efficacy of primary nursing as a foundation for patient advocacy. *Nursing Standard*, **5**, 2–5.

Chambers English Dictionary (1980) Macdonald, A.M. (ed.). W.R. Chambers, Edinburgh.

Concise Oxford Dictionary (1982) Sykes, J.B. (ed.). Oxford University Press, Oxford.

Department of Health (1989) *Caring For People*, HMSO, London.

Ford, R. and Ryan, P. (1992) Clinical mental health. Meeting needs with case management. *Nursing Standard*, **6**, 29–32.

Hale, C. (1993) *Nursing Development Unit and the Nursing Case Management Project*. Centre for Health Services Research, University of Newcastle Upon Tyne. Unpublished work.

Hancock, C. (1992a) *RCN Letter: Named Nurse*. RCN, London.

Hancock, C. (1992b) The named nurse concept. *Nursing Standard*, **16**, 16–18.

Hunt, J. (1988) Clinical primary nursing. The next challenge. *Nursing Times*, **84**, 36–8.

Iyer, P.A., Taptich, B.J. and Bernocchi-Losey, D. (1991) *Nursing Process and Nursing Diagnosis. W.B. Saunders Co, Philadelphia*.

Kemp, N. (1983). Quality Assurance and the Nursing Process. Florence Nightingale/Smith & Nephew Scholarship Report. The Florence Nightingale Committee, London.

Lear, G., Morris, G., Parnel, M. and Wharne, S. (1991) Case management: responding to the need. *Nursing Times*, **87**, 24–26.

Manthey, M. (1973). Primary nursing is alive and well in hospital. *American Journal of Nursing*, **1**, 83–82.

Manthey, M. (1988). Myths that threaten. What primary nursing really is. *Nursing Management*, **19**, 54–56.

Royal College of Nursing (1992) *Issues in Nursing and Health. Approaches to Nursing Care*, Paper 13. RCN, London.

United Kingdom Central Council (1989) *Exercising Accountability*. Advisory Document. UKCC, London.

United Kingdom Central Council (1992) *Code of Professional Conduct*, UKCC, London.

Wright, S. (1992) The named nurse. A question of accountability. *Nursing Times*, **88**, 27–29.

Zander, K. (1988) Nursing case management: Stategic management of cost quality outcomes. *Journal of Nursing Administration*, **18**, 23–30.

3

Assessment

In the last chapter we discussed the variety of ways in which care may be organised. There was no intention to be didactic in our approach but rather to confirm our belief that the named nurse concept is a good one.

When people become ill and require nursing intervention then the first and most important task of the nurse is to assess the health state of that person in order to plan the necessary care. Assessment means 'the estimation of the size or quality of' (*Concise Oxford Dictionary*, 1992) and an assessor is someone who is called on to judge or give value to something (*Chambers English Dictionary*, 1988). It is not possible to make an accurate judgement, professional or otherwise, of another person without being able to communicate with them. Good communication is important at all stages in the patient's care but the earlier contact is made, the more effective it will be.

It is important for the nurse to develop good communication and interpersonal skills to be effective in any interview situation with patients. It is important for all nurses to develop self-awareness skills so that they may reduce some of the barriers to communication. Effective nursing requires a total acceptance that there is a multitude of differing lifestyles and that it is not our business to be judgemental of how other people may choose to live. Our concern arises when there is a recognised need for nursing intervention.

There are many books already available which detail communication and interpersonal skills in nursing. It is our intention only to highlight some of those areas which we feel are vital in good practice. Barbara Scammel (1990), in her book on communication skills, makes reference to the qualities needed in the good communicator. She speaks of the need for respect for others, for sincerity and a desire to help. The nurse should have a warm, caring personality and patience in listening.

A succint definition of communication by Russel and Bateson is cited by Sundeen *et al.* (1989). It refers to communication as 'all of the procedures by which one mind may affect another'. Later, they also refer to it as 'all verbal and non-verbal messages between participants'. They conclude that communication is not just a 'behavioural manifestation of a concept "relationship" but it is the relationship'. In the therapeutic relationship which develops between nurse and patient, the skills of listening and silence are as important as those conveying and exchanging information.

It may be helpful to the nurse to be reminded of the characteristics of the helping relationship as described by Carl Rogers, (1990). He feels that the helper should be seen as trustworthy and dependable; someone who portrays themselves openly and without ambiguity. The nurse should always be able to receive the other person as he is; she should be sensitive enough not to allow the client to feel in any way threatened or criticised.

The initial interview between nurse and patient is vitally important. In it the nurse needs to collect data from which an accurate assessment of the patient's health status can be made. This will be the crux of the whole process of enabling his needs to be met and his problems to be solved or helped. The patient's input to this process is vitally important, but in order to gain his confidence we need to give him information too. The importance of this partnership between patient and nurse cannot be emphasised too strongly. We cannot expect the patient to disclose to us information of a confidential nature if we have not told him why it is needed. In their *Position Statement on Nursing,* the RCN state that:

> Each patient has a right to be a partner in his own care planning and receive information, support and encouragement from the nurse which will permit him to make an informed choice and become involved in his own care.

(RCN, 1987)

The first meeting between nurse and client can set the tone of the whole relationship. This, and the subsequent assessment interview, should as far as possible be carefully preplanned. Clearly in an emergency situation this is not possible but the same principles should always be considered. At such a time it is particularly important to consider the effects of a sudden and upsetting change not just to the patient but also to the family or friends who may accompany him. Initial communication with them is as important as that with the patient and of course if the patient is unconscious then it is vital.

The venue for this meeting must be chosen with care with the criteria of privacy and preservation of dignity paramount. Remember how important it is to raise the patient's self esteem and to do nothing which would in any way lower it. It is possible to create an area of calm and quiet, relatively unobstructed by other people and things, even if that area is more in the mind than physically determined.

There must be structure to the interview. It has a beginning and ending, clearly defined and should logically progress, giving meaning to both participants. Integral to its development should be consideration of patient perceptions and expectations. We are on familiar territory doing a job with which we are comfortable. He may be in pain and distress, in unfamiliar surroundings and wondering why we are talking and not doing something. There may be urgent patient needs which have to be met before further communication can continue.

The conduct of the interview may be enhanced in two ways. It will be helpful to the nurse to have consulted the medical documentation available regarding the patient as this will give her cues to the direction and possible nature of the patient's problems. The information gained this way will act as a focus and point of reference.

Earlier it was suggested that using a model is also helpful as a frame of reference. It may be one of the nurse's own design but it is helpful to give structure to the questions and it does ensure that no important area of concern is omitted. Many clinical settings use activities of living (Roper *et al.*, 1990) as a framework for the assessment interview, but it does not always follow that this is the best or only way to make an exhaustive enquiry. Such a list may not always clearly identify the important areas of psychological and social need.

Questions need to be well thought out and formulated so that they elicit the desired response. The language the nurse uses is important; jargon and inappropriate medical terminology should be avoided. The moment chosen to ask the 'difficult' question must be skilfully and sensitively identified.

The conduct of the interview is vital. The skills mentioned before must be well honed. Remember that we are treading on private and personal ground. People tell nurses things they would not normally divulge even to their closest relative. Disclosure is painful and information gained in this way must be sensitively handled.

In an attempt to emphasise the importance of good communication in the nurse's repertoire of assessment skills it is all too easy to forget the need to be equally effective in observation. At one time this was the skill often identified as the most important of all and which the nurse 'perfected' as she became more experienced at her craft. By reminding ourselves of the importance of this we encourage nurses to focus on looking at the person rather than the machines to which they may be attached or to the nursing records which may be used as a reference.

It is not possible to communicate well without using the non-verbal as well as the verbal information which patients are presenting us with. As the nurse reads the messages that a combination of those two facets provide she should take note of the wider more clinical information that may be gleaned from the patient's physical state.

Clinical observation means using all the senses to gain information which may not be available in any other way and which, if not considered, may result in some serious omission in the achievement of an accurate picture of the patient's condition.One cannot stress too much the importance of correct identification of problems; the accuracy of care planning and subsequent nursing intervention rely on this.

Visual observation is particularly important to interpret the spoken word correctly. Not only does it give information about the way the individual presents himself to the world but also allows account to be taken of facial expressions and behavioural responses to the interactions taking place, all of which helps to make sense of the spoken communication.

Observation also allows the nurse to identify more physical phenomena such as the presence of unusual swellings or discoloration of the skin. It may point to features which require further investigation, for example, the significance of a bandage on the ankle. Many important physical details may also be discovered in this way, some or all of which may have clinical significance.

Listening does not simply allow us to hear what the patient says but also to hear and identify problems related to the respiratory system, e.g. are the respirations unduly noisy? Are they characterised by wheezing? Is there a productive cough?

Modern nurses are concerned to make use of touch in a therapeutic way and it is certainly important that this is considered in terms of helping and caring but it must not be forgotten that touch also allows us to discover changes in physical phenomena which again may have importance in both nursing and medical diagnosis. The nurse who observes the patient's swollen ankles should also discover if that swelling is oedema.

It is less likely that the senses of smell and taste are used as frequently in the assessment of a patient but there are instances where these too play a significant part. A particular odour may alert an experienced nurse to suspect the need for laboratory tests on a wound exudate.

There are of course also a number of instruments which nurses commonly employ in the collection of data. These should be used selectively and not always routinely; other information already gleaned should direct the nurse to the range of further tests needed. Laboratory analysis of body tissues and fluids also are an important aid to full assessment but are medically determined. However, the nurse may, for example, decide to carry out a Glucometer test on a known or suspected diabetic.

The assessment of patients often implies obtaining a picture of how the patient is at the moment of the interview but there are often situations where it is also important that the nurse discovers how the patient lived before he became ill enough to require nursing intervention. This is particularly important when considering goal setting as it may be totally unrealistic to aim for optimum function when it was not present before the present health problem appeared. That does not mean, however, that there is no need to consider other than the present problem but rather that this knowledge has to be taken into the whole picture in the planning phase.

This first interview enables the nurse to obtain a baseline of information against which new and changing information can be compared. Normally one never again needs to repeat the detailed initial assessment because the sequential nature of the nursing process allows the nurse to deal with changing circumstances. However, the long-stay patient may require new information added to the original assessment, particularly where social relationships and circumstances may change and thus affect discharge planning. The elderly patient may lose a spouse, or a supportive wife may herself become ill and unable to provide expected care. In the spinal unit, during the course of recovery from initial injury, the young man may find his partner unable to cope with his changed image and even a 'permanent' relationship may be broken. His inability to work may lead to repossession of a mortgaged property and housing becomes a greater problem than before. Any significant change such as that indicated must be dated and signed when added to the document.

Just as it was important to begin the interview well, so the conclusion must also be handled effectively. It helps to summarise and check the information which has been collected. It is not helpful to have made wrong assumptions; after all, the patient's future care depends on it. It may also be the case that the information gathered is incomplete, either because the patient was not well enough to continue the interview or because it was inappropriate to examine certain physical aspects of the patients problems at the time. The nurse has a responsibility to ensure that the fact does not go unrecognised and a mechanism is in place to ensure that the document is duly completed. The patient needs to be assured of the use to which the data will be put.He also needs an opportunity to ask questions of the nurse. There may be innumerable things which are troubling him. During the course of the interview the nurse must enable the patient to feel free and comfortable to ask questions knowing that he will be neither rebuffed nor ridiculed.

Before leaving the patient, tell him what will happen next, particularly when he clearly has a problem which needs rather rapid resolution.

There may be times when it is not possible to obtain vital information from the patient directly; he may be unconscious or unable to speak clearly, if at all. In such situations the appropriate details will have to be obtained from relatives or friends. The same skills of communication are as important in those situations as with the patient himself in order that an accurate picture may be obtained. The nurse must, however, bear in mind that information gained in this way may require rather different interpretation from that which is subjectively acquired. Note should be made in the record of the name and relationship of the person who gave the information. This is important as conflicting information may be given by people whose relationship with the patient may vary.

Good communication and observation are the two skills which allow nurses to make accurate assessments of individuals. It is the responsibility of the patient's named nurse to ensure that this assessment has been carried out and the information obtained collated and documented in such a way that the subsequent plan of care is the best possible. The first stage of planning involves the correct identification of the patient's problems and needs.

References

Chambers English Dictionary. (1988) MacDonald, A.M. (ed.). W.R. Chambers, Edinburgh.

The Concise Oxford Dictionary. (1992) Allen, R.A. (ed.). Oxford University Press, Oxford.

Rogers, C.R. (1990) *On Becoming a Person.* Constable, London.

Roper, N., Logan, W. and Tierney, A. (1990) *The Elements of Nursing,* 3rd edn. Churchill Livingstone, Edinburgh.

Royal College of Nursing (1987) *Position Statement on Nursing.* RCN, London.

Scammel, B. (1990) *Communication Skills.* Macmillan, London.

Sundeen, S.J., Stuart, G.W., Rankin, E.A.D. and Cohen, S. (1989) *Nurse–Client Interaction: Implementing the Nursing Process,* 4th edn. C.V. Mosby, St Louis.

4

Problem identification

Having discussed the factors relevant to the assessment interview, we now go on to discuss the identification of the patients nursing problems. We have emphasised our belief that good nursing care is a partnership between the patient and nurse. The patient gives the information and the nurse makes judgements.

Having identified the problems the nurse consults the patient, telling him of her findings, gauging his feelings and establishing what he thinks are his main problems. This not only lets the patient know that his opinions and wishes are of consequence, but it is also a means of confirming the existence and precise nature of his problems. Often patients will identify something the nurse has failed to pick up and this is often very important to him. However, the patient may see something as normal that appears a problem to the health care staff. Such problems may be those that offend against society or are dangerous to himself and others, for example alcohol abuse or being a heavy smoker. Some unacknowledged problems may be the result of lack of information and/or understanding or illness. It is part of the nurse's role to give to the patient information that will enable him to understand his problem/s. Conversely, the patient may help the nurse to avoid identifying problems that do not exist. The patient also needs information in order to be involved, to be able to contribute to his care and to be able to take part in identifying and subsequently reaching the goals of care, if he so wishes.

Whilst we choose to use the term *problem*, some nurses use the word *need* and at times the words are used interchangeably. Needs can be defined as something of necessity without necessarily being a problem. A patient's problem may be defined as something the patient cannot cope with which requires a solution. A patient's nursing care problem is one that requires nursing intervention.

A quote from Little and Carnevali (1976) that the reader may find useful is:

Areas of nursing diagnosis (nursing care problems) are related to, but distinct from medicine. Where medicine labels symptoms and pathology, nursing describes the effects of these symptoms and pathology on the activities and the style of living now and in the future.

Problems are listed on the patient's nursing care plan. The problem list is an itemisation of the problems which the nurse has discovered from the data collected from and about the patient. As Bowers (1972) points out, problems arise when the patient, family or community:

a)   cannot meet a need;
b)   need help in meeting a need;
c)   are not aware of an unmet need;
d)   have conflict of apparently equal needs;
e)   must choose from several alternative ways of meeting needs.

cited by McFarlane & Castledine (1982)

Problems may be listed under two headings: actual and potential.

Actual problems are those that exist, whether the patient is aware of them or not. Examples include:

- vomiting of unknown cause
- loss of faith due to sudden bereavement
- feelings of anxiety
- hallucination
- poor coordination of movement
- loneliness

Potential problems are those that the patient is at risk of developing as a result of his medical or social condition. Problem statements should always be prefixed by the word 'potential' and a reason for the problem included. Sometimes a patient will be admitted to hospital with no actual nursing care problems, for example when admitted for a series of medical tests. However, he may have some potential problems. Nurses identify the potential problems, to try to help the patient prevent the problem occurring or to help him cope with complications of his condition. The potential problem list could be endless, so it is sensible to include those most likely to occur, such as those that could be life threatening and those that call for nursing involvement. Examples include:

- bleeding due to anticoagulant therapy
- hypoglycaemia due to reluctance to take adequate meals
- skin damage due to loss of sensation
- risk of developing deep vein thrombosis
- risk of airway obstruction due to local swelling of tongue
- risk of alcohol withdrawal symptoms.

Identifying problems is not easy, it calls for experience and knowledge about nursing. It requires empathy for the patient and intellectual skills including the ability to analyse and synthesise the information. To do this effectively the nurse reviews the assessment information and weighs up the evidence, including any she has gleaned from other sources. She has to be conscious of any discrepancies and/or inconsistencies in the information. She analyses the facts, including the impressions she received during the assessment interview and when talking to the patient afterwards. She looks for connection between the pieces of information. She should reflect back on previous situations which may stimulate her thinking further. She should also think ahead and consider the patient's likely outcome of care, for example, any problems he may have on being discharged from hospital. There may also, of course, be a need to recheck some facts. Some problems may not be disclosed by the patient and may only be identified when the patient and nurse relationship develops and the patient trusts the nurse.

A nursing model can be useful when attempting to identify a patient's nursing care problems, because it enables the nurse to focus on the patient as a whole, and then on specific components of the model. However, a more simple way of identifying problems is to consider the following: what is happening to the patient physiologically? socially? psychologically? spiritually? and how are the patient and those close to him coping? Also consider what was normal for the patient before his admission to health care. Is it likely he can ever return to his previous lifestyle? As Mayers (1978) says:

> To identify a discrepancy in a patient's situation it is necessary 1) to know what is expected at a given point in time, 2) to make a valid assessment of the actual situation, and 3) to come to a conclusion as to the consequences of any differences between desired and actual status.

We have often found it helpful to review the general impression of the patient. For example, Mr Jones is a 60-year-old retired school teacher. He is a bachelor and lives alone. He looks unhappy and admits he cannot be bothered to cook food for himself. He has an old dog, Bessie, of whom he is very fond. He says he is worried she will fret whilst he is away. A neighbour is looking after the dog. Mr Jones used to enjoy walking but now he cannot be bothered. Mr Jones has been admitted for investigations of cardiac arrhythmias which are being monitored. He doesn't admit to any worries or difficulties, apart from missing Bessie and being 'a bit worried about having palpitations'.

Already one can list a number of possible problems; however, having made the list it is necessary to see whether the facts support the identification and whether they need to be checked before discussing them with Mr Jones.

One may be tempted to think Mr Jones is unhappy or lonely but let us consider the facts. He looks unhappy but it may be his usual expression without indicating that anything is wrong. It is wrong to judge a person's mood just by a facial expression. He cannot be bothered to cook for himself or to go out for walks; this too could indicate a lonely or unhappy person or does it? On looking further at the assessment data (or later when discussing the possible problems with Mr Jones) the nurse might find out that he does not know how to cook, because he has always eaten in the school canteen or in hotels during holidays. He does not walk much because his palpitations get worse if he walks even a short distance. He does have some friends but he loves Bessie best (a number of pet owners like their animals better than people). What we are trying to demonstrate here is that whilst it is useful to get an overview of the patient, because it helps us see him as an individual, it also helps trigger the problem solving activity and often identifies a number of problems. However, we must not jump to conclusions; a problem may not be as it seems. Interpretation of the facts needs careful consideration. This is particularly so when the facts are scarce or when dealing with emotional or subjective information. If there is any doubt, recheck the facts, preferably with the patient or, if appropriate, with those significant to him, and the medical notes or previous nursing notes.

When identifying problems, write down the obvious such as those identified by the patient at the assessment; for example, 'Worried how husband will cope alone, he is 79 years old'. Write down those problems which can be identified by the senses; for example, 'Sore mouth, Confused in time and place. Skin hot and dry, Ulcers give off unpleasant odour'. Then analyse and synthesise the facts that remain.

Nurses should never be afraid to seek advice from colleagues. When appropriate they should use research findings to aid accurate problem identification or to support the need to write down a problem.

Some authors suggest that the problem is written from the patient's perspective and in the patients words. However, we have to be realistic; it is not always easy to quote the patient directly. Sometimes the patient will not accept he has a problem (this in itself can be a problem!). He may not have the knowledge or understanding to appreciate the significance of what is happening to him. He may be too ill or too tired to want to be involved. The solution seems to be to quote the patient where possible, but only if the quotation gives a clear indication of the problem. Examples identified by patients:

- 'only sleep on and off during the night, reading helps'
- 'wake up dripping in sweat'
- 'food has no taste'
- 'unable to pick up small things'
- 'tend to get constipated'

'No visitors to be allowed in, that includes the wife and daughter'. Mr Green does not wish to give a reason.

When writing down the problem stated by the patient, put the statement in inverted commas. There may be a need to add a statement, to the one made by Mr Green. It may not seem like a problem for him, but the nurses, and perhaps Mr Green, may have to deal with any repercussion. The nurses may have to help Mr Green cope with his decision.

If it is not possible to quote the patient, make a statement that is clearly understood, if possible including the cause of the problem, for example:

Frequent offensive diarrhoea due to ulcerative colitis.
Unable to speak, leftsided stroke on 1/8/92.
Unable to swallow due to oesophageal obstruction.
Is noisy at night, does not know where he is.
Painful joints in hands due to rheumatoid arthritis.

It can be very misleading if problems are not correctly identified. Sometime nurses use jargon and emotive terminology or unnecessary medically oriented language, for example, 'needs assistance with mobilising', 'needs tender loving care', 'racked with grief', 'unstable diabetic'. These terms could have a variety of interpretations and could stem from a number of possibilities. If a problem statement is ambiguous the right care may not be planned.

It has to be accepted that the nurse may place problems in a different order of importance from that of the patient. For example, a patient was admitted to a neurological ward for tests. The nurse, having identified the problems, put them in order of priority. However, the only problem the patient had identified and had referred to twice in the conversation was bottom of the nurse's list. The patient insisted that the problem of claustrophobia be put first – she had a very real fear of the MRI scan that was planned for the next day. The nurse's prescription was reassurance. The patient asked if she could walk to see the machine (it was in the same building). She also asked if she could be given some form of tranquilliser – the latter met with obvious disapproval and it was refused. The patient then asked the doctor for a small dose of tranquilliser before undergoing the scan which he readily agreed to (she had never needed tranquillisers in the past). This prescription was added to the care plan at the patient's request, but she kept worrying it would be forgotten – it was not. Despite the kindness and care of the radiographer the patient found it very difficult to stay in the machine for the 45 minutes the scan took. She subsequently found out that in that hospital, 10 per cent of the patients did not cope with the claustrophobia experienced whilst in the machine. If the nurse conducting the assessment had listened carefully and been aware of the failure rate of people attending the MRI scan she could have lessened the patient's stress and perhaps been a more effective nurse for the knowledge.

It is sometimes difficult to separate the patient's nursing care problems from the medical diagnosis, because they often overlap. The patient's nursing care problems are those requiring nursing action but nurses may need to refer to other disciplines for help or the care may overlap. For example, when obtaining dietary advice, the dietitian usually writes their advice on the patient's care plan – they may redefine the problem in conjunction with the nurse and/or doctor. There may be an occasion where the nurse has to take a secondary role; for example, when a patient requires intensive exercise. The programme is planned and may be supervised by the physiotherapist with the nurse taking over in the physiotherapist's absence. A difficulty may arise as to where to write such problems and the action to be taken. The physiotherapist may choose to write on the nursing care plan or they may add the problem to the physiotherapy notes. We feel that if a nurse refers to a patient's problem she must write it down on the patient's nursing care plan and encourage the paramedical staff to write any instructions to be carried out by the nurses on that patient's nursing care plan.

Problem statements should be legible and stated precisely, leaving no room for misinterpretation. Each problem should be dated the day it was written on the care plan; the date will be significant when reviewing and evaluating the patient's care. When a problem ceases to be a problem it should be crossed through with a fine line to enable the words underneath to be seen and an evaluation statement written.

We could have referred to nursing diagnosis in this chapter but we have chosen to discuss the subject in Chapter 9 where we consider, amongst other things, the costing of nursing work.

Part of quality care for patients involves the correct identification of the problems they may have or could develop. If the problem is not correctly identified the planning of care may be misdirected and the outcome poor or even dangerous. It behoves nurses to identify problems accurately.

References

Bower, F.L. (1972) *The Process of Planning Care*, C.V. Mosby, St Louis.

McFarlane, Baroness of Llandaff and Castledine, G. (1982) *A Guide to the Practice of Nursing using the Nursing Process.* C.V. Mosby, London.

Mayers, M.G. (1978) *A Systematic Approach to the Nursing Care Plan.* 2nd edn. Appleton-Century-Crofts, New York.

Little, D.E. and Carnevali, D.L. (1976) *Nursing Care Planning*, 2nd edn. J.B. Lippincott, Philadelphia.

5

The process of goal setting

Once the problem has been identified the next stage is to set appropriate goals. The definition of a goal can be a point marking the end of a race; an object of effort or ambition; destination. (*Concise Oxford Dictionary*, 1982). A more detailed explanation of a goal in relation to patient care may be:

> A goal is a statement of a desired, achievable outcome to be attained within a predicted period of time, given the presenting situation and resources.
>
> (Little and Carnevali, 1976)

A goal means what a person will be doing as a result of care and/or treatment which is different and better than at present (Lunt, 1986).

Whilst we have chosen to use the word *goal*, many other nurses use *objective, desired outcome, expected outcome* and *target*. All these words can be said to have the same meaning when referring to nursing care. Little and Carnevali (1976) refer to the words patients may use when discussing the goals of care; some of these are *hopes, aims, wants, wishes, purposes* and *ambitions*. This is a useful list to remember when discussing goals of care with the patient.

A goal statement should contain:

1. an *observation* of something that the patient expresses or behaviour that he will be able to do;
2. a *measurement* and *time constraint* that enables an evaluation of the patient's progress and care to be carried out;

and it should be achievable and appropriate for the patient and the resources available.

Formulating and writing goals appears to give many people difficulty for too often, as Lunt (1978) points out, 'Goals are implicit or intuitive, rather than explicit, which can leave others in the dark, including the patient'. Often goals are written as aims, or what Mager (1975) calls 'fuzzies'. We have all seen such examples: 'to be mobilised', 'wound to heal', 'to be rehydrated', 'to have quality of life'. There is nothing wrong in principle with these statements; they often reflect the philosophy of the people writing them. However, they are almost impossible to measure and evaluate effectively.

Goals should contain a statement about some activity the patient will carry out or that will occur as a result of care or therapy. As we suggested in the last chapter before writing the goal statements, the nurse should discuss the problems with the patient. She should ask, when appropriate to do so, what sort of change the patient would like to see as a result of the care he is going to receive. Together they will discuss how the goal is to be achieved and the kind of nursing action and treatment that will take place to aid the achievement of the goal.

Whilst the nurse, through her knowledge, experience and analysis of the assessment data, can guide the goal setting it is only after discussion with the patient or significant others that his resources can be identified to enable him to reach the goal. 'Resources' in this context means the help he is likely to give or obtain from others, such as family, friends or the support services, for without such help it is unlikely that some goals will be achieved.

However, not all patients can or wish to be involved in identifying their problems or needs, let alone the setting of goals. Where the patient lacks the ability to be involved and has no-one to speak for him, the nurse, as indicated earlier, takes on this role. To involve the patient who is disinterested and/or unwilling to be involved is also difficult.

In most situations the nurse's relationship with the patient and her skill may enable her to overcome some of the difficulties. But whatever the circumstances, the nurse still has to capitalise on any strengths the patient may have or has had.

One of the advantages of goal setting is that it can act as a stimulus for the patient – something that gives him a sense of purpose, something to work for. For example: Mr John Brown, a patient with bone metastasis, was at home receiving terminal care. He was being cared for by his wife, Anne, and the district nurse. He had become withdrawn and was apparently not interested in anything and said as much. He just wanted 'to get it over with'. Anne and the nurse discussed how they could help him. Anne said that he had been a keen gardener until recently. It was suggested to John that he plan a flower garden with Anne and supervise her carrying out the work. This they did together. He sat in a chair whilst she dug the garden and planted the seeds. There is no doubt that these activities, which were achieved through a series of goal steps, enabled the patient to reach the goal, 'Planned and supervised the planting of a flower garden by 21 March, 1988'.

This example shows how, by discussing a problem and identifying a patient's strengths (in this case his love for his wife and his past interest), it was possible to motivate the patient and give him and his wife something to work for, which obviously helped them both. It also enabled the patient, his wife and the nurse to plan other goals

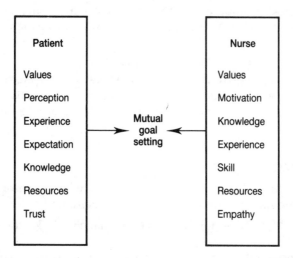

Fig. 5.1   Factors influencing mutual goal setting

Writing a goal statement (Based on Mager, 1975)

A goal may contain the following:

1. *Performance* – the actual behaviour, communication or clinical features demonstrated by the patient, e.g. walks; recognises; writes; reports; decreasing weight.
2. *Condition* – the environment or help required from a person and or resources, e.g. with the aid of the Zimmer frame; supported by daughter; in the hall.
3. *Criteria* – the measurement of how well, how long, how far, how often, how much, e.g. walks with the Zimmer frame from the hall to the door twice a day; loss of weight – 1 kg in one week.
4. *Target* – the predicted time by which the goal will be achieved and thus evaluated.
5. *Review* – a checking time may be necessary for some long term goals, when an evaluation statement should also be written.

Goals may be classified according to three types of time constraint: immediate, short term and long term.

Immediate

An immediate goal would be necessary for such situations as pre-operative and postoperative care, diabetic coma, seizures, etc. The goal may be written in minutes/hours, according to the patient's condition, for example:

Problem: potential shock, following operation.
Goals could include: warm, dry skin; stable blood pressure 130/80 – 140/90 mmHg; pulse rate 60–90 beats per minute, regular and strong; resting quietly; no bright red, blood-saturated dressing. Review every 15 minutes.

Short term

A short term goal is used for any situation where a resolution of the problem can more or less be predicted, for example:

Problem: 1.2.93. As a newly diagnosed diabetic, lacks the skill to test urine.
Goal: demonstrate correct method of testing urine using clinistix, recording and reporting results accurately by 3.2.93.

Long term

The length of time may be weeks or even months for psychological, social, spiritual and chronic physical problems, for example: breakdown in relationships, abnormal grief reaction, alcohol dependence, loneliness, bizzare behaviour, loss of vision and varicose ulcers.

When setting goals for the long-term problem, it is advisable to break them down into manageable parts. These are usually referred to as goal steps or subgoals and can be achieved in a shorter space of time than the long-term goal.

From the patient's point of view he is much more likely to be interested in working towards something he can see is achievable in a short space of time, rather than the long-term goal which could be reached some time in the future. In this way, too, the patient will be working at a pace in keeping with his predicted progress.

As a goal step is achieved the nurse and, if possible, the patient will together evaluate progress so far and discuss the feasibility of moving on to the next step. Goal steps therefore not only help to motivate the patient but ensure that evaluation is systematically carried out at pre-determined intervals. This is a more effective procedure than waiting for the achievement of the long term goal or for something unexpected to happen.

How many goal steps do you write? There are no hard or fast rules

– it depends on the patient, his condition and the resources available, together with the nurse's skill and experience in dealing with the particular problem. Goal steps for some problems can more or less be predicted, as in the example given below. However, for the more protracted problem, it can at times be difficult to predict the time span for the achievement of the long-term goal or even the goal steps required. Therefore it is sensible to write only one or two goal steps to be achieved in a specific time. As progress is evaluated and goals are achieved, further goal steps may be written. Thus, subgoals or goal steps may be written as illustrated in the following example.

Mr Brian Smith is a 72-year-old married man. He lives with his wife who is devoted to him. A married daughter lives close by. Six months ago Mr Smith suffered a stroke which left him with a right-sided hemiplegia. He made a good recovery and was discharged from hospital four months ago. His wife says he has recently become reluctant to use his walking aid following a slight fall.

The care plan below shows the various goal steps used for Mr Smith. If we remember to involve the patient and his family in problem identification and the setting of goal steps, the outcome is more likely to be successful.

Care plan for Mr Smith

Date	Problem	Goals
1.2.93	Reluctant to walk using walking aid following slight fall (has right-sided hemiplegia)	Walks from armchair to sitting room door twice each day on his own using a Zimmer frame. Review 13.2.93
		Walks from armchair to front door twice each day using Zimmer frame. Review 20.2.93
		States he is confident to walk to shop with his wife by 26.2.93
		Walks to shop using Zimmer frame and accompanied by his wife Tuesday and Friday. Review 5.3.93
		Walks to daughter's home for tea and returns without difficulty. Review 12.3.93
		Resumes routine of walking to shop and visiting daughter – using walking aid. By 1.4.93

Some nurses may choose to use the patient's name when writing goals. However, if the care plan is centred on the patient, is this necessary? Nevertheless, at times the person giving help will need to be named, for example: Accepts daughter's help to get in and out of bath.

All goals must have a *performance*. This can be the observed 'patient behaviour' or activity, i.e. what he reports or says, what he does. It may also be a clinical manifestation which is not necessarily under the control of the patient, such as normal temperature, weight loss, decreasing decubitus ulcer. A goal statement carries more impact if it starts with a verb: states, demonstrates, listens, smiles, writes, reduces, contrasts, selects, washes. It is not always necessary to write a condition for a goal, for example:

Problem: 1.4.93, dry mouth.
Goal: Clean moist buccal mucosa by 2.4.93.

A goal statement must also have a *criterion*, for this is the indicator for evaluating how effective the care of the patient has been and how he has responded to that care. It is also worth noting that the writing of measurable goals should enable nurses to be more effective when they set and measure nursing standards.

The target date

This is the predicted time when the goal will be achieved and an evaluation made and written. It will be in part influenced by the nurse's knowledge and experience and the patient's condition, motivation and resources. It must be realistic, meaning the patient should be able to achieve the goal by the stated time. Some target dates are not easy to predict, as we said earlier, particularly with long-term goals; however, if they are broken down into manageable parts (goal steps) this problem can be overcome.

It may on occasion be necessary to set a review date, a time when progress is checked and a statement written. To set a date, be this target or review, is essential, for this is a specific and disciplined way of ensuring care is evaluated.

Some further examples of problems and goals which the nurse may find helpful are given on page 43. However, it should be remembered that goals are individual to patients because of their particular needs and resources. It does not follow that the type of problem stated here will necessarily have the goals we have set.

Date	Problem	Goals
1.3.93	Potential bleeding due to predicted long term administration of warfarin tablets.	Lists accurately the side effects and action to be taken on 3.3.93. States he can cope if side effects occur. By 3.3.93.
1.3.93	Potential hypoglycaemic attacks due to instability of blood glucose level (newly diagnosed diabetic)	Experiences hypoglycaemic attack under controlled conditions. By 2.3.93 Lists correctly actions to prevent and deal with hypoglycaemic attack. By 3.3.93. States he is confident to deal with hypoglycaemia after discharge from hospital. By 5.3.93.
1.3.93	Passing hard, dry stools twice weekly	Regains normal bowel action and pattern of once daily. By 7.3.93.
1.3.93	Outbursts of verbal and physical aggression at least twice every hour	Time between outbursts extended to two hours. Review daily. Target date 5.3.93.
1.3.93	Disorientated with regard to time	Accurately reports to primary nurse each morning the date, time and place. Review daily
1.3.93	Overweight by 12.5 kg. (awaiting cardiac surgery)	Reduce weight by 3 kg first week – 7.3.93. Reduce weight thereafter by 1.5kg weekly. Review weekly. Achieves target weight of 85 kg. By 5.4.93

References

Concise Oxford Dictionary (1982) Sykes, J.B. (ed.). Oxford University Press, Oxford.

Little, D.E. and Carnevali, D.L. (1976) *Nursing Care Planning*, 2nd edn. J.B. Lippincott, Philadelphia.

Lunt, B.J. (1978)*The Goal Setting Approach in Continuing Care*. Paper presented at Annual Therapeutic Conference, St Christopher's Hospice, Sydenham, 17 November 1993.

Lunt, B.J. (1986) Terminal Care: Goal setting – Hospice Philosophy in Practice. *Current Issues in Clinical Practice*. Vol 3, (ed) Karas E. Plenum.

Mager, R.F. (1975) *Preparing Instructional Objectives*, 2nd edn. Fearnon Pitman, Belmont, California.

6

Planning and implementation

Once the goals of nursing care have been determined and priorities have been agreed then decisions have to be made by the nurse about the actions which are needed to achieve the goals. In reaching such decisions the nurse has to take account of the resources which are available to her in terms of staff, equipment, time and finance where it is applicable. This involves the nurse in careful planning.

As with all other stages of the process ideally decisions should be taken with the full involvement of the patient. The patient does not usually have the degree of insight into the possibilities or alternative methods of achieving the stated goals, nor does he have the nursing knowledge and experience to call on but he does have the right to be consulted and make an informed decision about the care he will receive.

In considering options and making choices about care the nurse will draw on her own experience and the knowledge which she has gained from her reading and consultation with other professionals. It is helpful if decisions can be made from the basis of research which has been carried out by nurses who have used a scientific approach to examining nursing practice. Every time a nurse makes a nursing decision she should be able to offer a rationale for her actions. 'A nurse who is unable to give a reason for nursing actions is practising irresponsibly' (Sundeen *et al.*, 1989). The UKCC *Code of Professional Conduct* (1992) reminds us 'to maintain and improve . . . professional knowledge and competence'. This should be reflected in the quality of our decision-making and in our ability to clearly justify our care planning.

Just as the nurse takes the client's own wishes and feelings into account in making decisions about care, so she might consult with other health care professionals before finalising her plan. It would clearly be foolish to create conflict by not acknowledging the important role that paramedical workers play in the care of the elderly rehabilitation patient for example. Clients being cared for in the community can only receive maximum benefit from all available agencies if there has been collaboration between all appropriate team members in planning care. In community settings also, one might only be able to ensure that clients were receiving the best and most appropriate range of services from all available agencies if there was collaboration by all the team from the start. Not only is conflict avoided in this way but it also prevents the possibility that there may be duplication of care or that some vital service may be forgotten altogether.

This notion of collaborative care planning is becoming more common and is upheld in the letter of July 1992 from the Department of Health's Chief Nursing Officer when it is proposed that:

> The development of collaborative care plans between medical, nursing and therapy professionals contained within a single record to enhance the quality and consistency of care within hospital and between hospital and community should be encouraged.

There is no doubt that such a suggestion does make sense.

In most situations where nurses are considering a choice of actions it is useful to consider the full range of options which are available to her and her patient. This requires explicit evaluation of all the alternatives which her knowledge and experience offer her. It may be appropriate for some elderly patients to plan a habit training programme to promote continence of urine but this is not necessarily always the right or best method for everyone. It is interesting to note that Benner (1984), in her description of the 'expert' nurse, suggests she 'no longer relies on an analytic principle to connect her or his understanding of the situation to an appropriate action'; rather she 'has an intuitive grasp of each situation and zeroes in on the accurate region of the problem without wasteful consideration of a large range of unfruitful, alternative diagnoses and solutions.' These experts were, however, experienced and highly skilled clinicians and for the majority of practising nurses there is a need to be aware of alternatives at whatever level of conscious thought we consider them.

A consideration of alternatives emphasises the need for the nurse to be making decisions based on knowledge drawn from both biological and behavioural sciences. Scientific principles should be applied wherever possible. These are the bases on which medical decisions are made and our prescriptions must have a similar basis in deliberate and purposeful decisions which have been arrived at as a result of logical thinking.

Nursing actions are, of course, those which will enable the stated goals to be met. These must be kept clearly in mind as the nurse seeks clarity for her written instructions. As the goals have been set with the patient so must the actions to reach these goals be discussed with him. He may have his own ideas of what he wishes to do or he may have a relative or friend who has had a similar problem and was not happy with the way his care was planned. This may have given him very fixed ideas about things he does not wish to do. To this debate the nurse must bring her professional knowledge and with her already established relationship with the patient, negotiate the appropriate plan which will meet the stated outcomes, be acceptable to the patient and satisfy the nurse that it is professionally sound.

The previous discussion emphasises that, in writing the care plan the nurse is 'individualising' care. It is this which provides quality for the individual and as Carnevali (1983) suggests 'differentiates the nursing order from some other closely related plans for health care'.

Nurses very often make reference to and use standard care plans. These have a place in nursing practice but they are not individualised plans of care and should not be adopted wholesale. They are sometimes produced on printed cards, in looseleaf files or on a computer programme. As such they are good ways of communicating to staff expected actions in relation to investigations or surgery. They can be useful as guidelines to care planning for student nurses, newly appointed staff nurses or bank and agency nurses. Experienced nurses should have that information internalised and be able to recall such patterns of activity when creating individual care plans.

There are many disadvantages to using standard care plans, the first and most obvious one being that by their very nature they are not individually designed and therefore negate the many principles which we have already advocated. By drawing on something which is preplanned the nurse may omit to consider a problem which her patient has but which the care plan does not make allowance for. Some nurses insist that standard care plans can be individualised but there is always the temptation, when under stress, to accept it as it is without further consideration. It is likely that the nurse may become overfamiliar with the content of the plan and stop using her critical thinking skills to make decisions for her patient based on her specific assessment data.

In a similar vein nursing actions may be guided by locally set policies and procedures which may be helpful to the inexperienced nurse in framing the preferred actions to be taken. It is important,however, to state that the circumstances in which policies shoud be enforced should be very clear. Policies and procedures are formulated at a particular time and for a particular purpose; the situation which caused them to be written in the first place may change and there is a need to review and update from time to time.

Another area of difficulty arises when nurses are considering the inclusion of actions which are the result of medical planning and treatment. We do, of course, carry out activities which doctors have ordered but there needs to be a clear distinction in nurses' minds between those actions which are medically determined and those which are purely concerned with nursing management. To quote Carnevali (1983), nursing care and medical care are 'complimentary but not identical'. Carnevali (1983) also makes the point that it is in 'the "style" of carrying out the medical order or in the additional nursing actions that may accompany it' that the difference lies. An example of this may be the action the nurse prescribes on the care plan to prevent cross-infection when the doctor has ordered immunosuppressive drugs. Nursing interventions may also be needed when there are no obvious related medical actions. An elderly patient may suffer a bereavement while receiving medical treatment for an acute infection; the nursing action in this instance will be prescribed to enable the patient to deal with his sense of loss and would exist without relevant medical intervention.

From the discussion above it is obvious that writing nursing actions as with the other elements of nursing care planning requires a great deal of intellectual activity in terms of critical thinking and decision making.It takes time but it cannot be stated too firmly that the time taken is essential if activities are to be in the best interests of the patient and designed to enable individual goals to be met. Ideally, as with other elements of the care plan nursing actions must be patient centred and as stated earlier, discussed with the patient before being written onto the plan.

In writing the nursing instruction certain factors must be borne in mind. As one of the obvious reasons for the care plan document is to ensure good communication, it is essential that what is written is clear and cannot be misinterpreted. It should also be concise but not so brief that clarity of meaning is lost. As a number of nurses may carry out care from the same plan it is a good idea to check the initial written instruction with another professional. This is often a salutary experience, as what seemed to the writer a perfectly obvious statement may be anything but obvious to someone else.

As with other elements of the care plan each instruction should be dated and signed. It is anticipated that in the first instance the nurse responsible for the patient assessment will go on to complete the written plan. Instructions written at this time will probably require modification at a later date and the same principles must apply at every point.In reviewing care it always helps to be able to read through a logical sequence of events so that the pattern of the patient's need for nursing intervention is clearly seen.

When the nurse writes goals for patient problems she writes them in terms of what the patient can achieve; thus they are primarily client orientated; when writing nursing actions it is more likely that the written statement will be nurse orientated. That is not always the case and there are times when it is necessary to clearly identify just who is going to carry out the written instruction,

- e.g. Mr. Brown's wife will come in at 10am each day to assist with his bathing;

- The hairdresser will wash Miss Jones' hair once a week on Friday afternoons.

The reader will identify a number of other criteria from these statements that are important in the writing of nursing actions. Each statement includes an action verb and that verb should be quite precise in what it is asking the individual to do. Nurses are not always so precise and may be guilty of using verbs such as 'to reassure' which can be open to a wide range of interpretations. There are many instances where reassurance is important in nursing but it does have to be specified. Carnevali (1983) gives us some examples of questions the nurse might ask to determine what the writer means when this word is used

- stay with him?
- listen to him?
- touch him? refrain from touching?
- stay away so that he knows you trust him to take responsibility for himself?
- inform him of your belief in his capability?

It is important to remember this when writing.

There are also times when it helps to add an adverb to qualify the way in which the action may be performed, e.g. talk loudly, walk briskly, drink slowly.

Similarly, precision must be used in considering the timing element of the action. Does it occur once in the day or more often? Does the action occur every hour of the day and night or should it only happen during waking hours? If the latter is true then it would be sensible to specify between which hours precisely. It is not enough, either, to suggest merely that an action should occur every two hours as the starting point should be determined so that the statement should read 'every two hours on the odd or even hour'. This principle applies to other orders which are written to be carried out on a regular basis.

In the case of certain activities it is necessary that the nurse has clearly thought through the consequence of her written action in terms of the effects on the patient. There may be occasions when a patient is required to lie prone for certain periods of the day and it would not be sensible to write a plan which resulted in the patient being in that position at meal times nor when his visitors are likely to arrive if this can be avoided. In respect of timing consideration should also be given to the duration of any activity. In the case of the activity described above this may seem fairly obvious but it is just as necessary to be prescriptive in terms of other less likely activities such as time spent on teaching patients or on giving time to allow patients to express anxiety. This may be thought to be limiting but sometimes the patient is grateful just to know that there is time set aside for him. The sensitive nurse will know when there is a need for a flexible approach in this area.

In considering timing it may also be appropriate to consider whether there is a need to specify the number of times an activity should be repeated or a time limit on a given date for its cessation. Clearly in acute areas where there is a rapid change in patients' response and reaction to care, this may be inappropriate, but this is always an area worth considering. There are many nursing situations which parallel the medical prescription need to specify the duration of a course of antibiotics, for example.

This example is also worth considering in terms of the accountability of the nurse in the accurate prescription of care. We would not carry out a drug prescription which did not clearly identify the drug, the dose, the route of administration, the timing and, where appropriate, the duration of the course. Neither would we give drugs from a prescription which was not dated and signed, nor from one which was in any way illegible and yet we are not always so explicit in our demands of the nursing prescription.

Another dimension of planning where timing is also a feature is in the consideration of the 24 hour cycle of activity/non-activity. This involves the nurse in setting out a plan for the patient's day (and night) which takes account of the many activities which may be happening over this period of time. This will allow for periods of activity to be interspersed by periods of rest. It will allow meal times to be free from interruptions such as investigations or visits of paramedical staff. It is common practice on units such as rehabilitation or spinal injuries where patients are kept particularly busy but with foresight it could be profitably considered elsewhere.

There are clinical areas where it is not clear where the responsibility for writing the care plan lies. If we believe that nursing is important, which clearly we do, then there must be no doubt where this responsibility does lie. The more we are reliant on bank and agency staff in the running of our wards and the more the skill mix changes, resulting in fewer trained nurses on duty then the more we must be sure that the patient is still receiving quality nursing care. The Patient's Charter (DoH, 1991) will certainly help in ensuring that the patient has a named nurse who is the person making decisions about care and that these decisions are made with knowledge and understanding and with due consideration for all identified and relevant factors. One of the purposes for the introduction of the health care assistant is to free the registered nurse to give more direct care.

'The development of the nursing plan is . . . a knowledgeable, creative and intellectual activity' (Yura and Walsh, 1988) and the finished plan should reflect this. Many nurses feel that time spent in writing the plan could be spent in giving care, but care which is not planned and neither based on the identification of problems real or perceived nor directed to achieve outcomes to solve these problems may be misdirected and time lost in the end. If the patient knows that care has been planned for him, what is likely to happen and who to call on for help, he is likely to be more relaxed and less anxious.

The plan is written in words on a document generally designed for that purpose, unless it is incorporated in a problem orientated record used by a number of professionals. Although it seems obvious to indicate that the plan is presented in words, it is worth noting the experience of Carnevali (1983) who, in visiting areas where clients with learning difficulties were being cared for, saw pictorial nursing orders, indicating that other residents who were unable to read were involved in giving care to others, such as washing and dressing. Colour coded cards were used to indicate what a particular resident could or could not do.

The purpose of the care plan is to act as a means of communication between those planning and those carrying out the care. Yura and Walsh (1988) describe it as 'an effective medium for transmitting information for planned care in that all team members can accurately perceive and implement the care intended'. In order to provide this medium it must be available at all times to those who need to use it. That means not just members of the nursing team but also the patient and his relatives or friends if he so wishes. This raises the question of confidentiality, an issue discussed by Wright (1990) in his article 'Patients' access to nursing records'. He makes many important points regarding the positive results of allowing patients to have access to their nursing notes, not least in the increasing trust and thus confidence which patients then have in the organisation looking after them. If we are discussing what we write with the patient it does seem only natural that he should read what we have written. Wright recommends that 'Each unit should produce guidelines for nurses to follow'. His own cover 17 points which include statements about where the notes should be kept.

It seems odd that there should still be a debate today about whether or not the nursing notes should be at the patient's bedside. Wright suggests that the patient be given the decision of whether they should be at the bedside or not. Statement 15 says:

> If the patients wish to see the notes, but not keep them at the bedside with them (e.g. do not wish relatives to see them), then these can be kept at the nursing station, but brought out for the patient to see as wished.

There are times when sensitive issues may arise such as sexuality or substance abuse, so that the nurse may be unhappy or unsure about recording such information where others may see it. Wright suggests that this is something which can be 'discussed with the primary nurse, taking into account the patient's degree of acceptance'. Where there is honesty and trust between patient and nurse then such sensitive issues can be more easily discussed.

A study carried out by Wilkinson (1989) caused her to recommend 'that the most acceptable location for care plans is at the patient's bedside'. Her reasons for this decision were that:

1. more care as planned is carried out if they are kept at the bedside than if they are kept at the nurses' station;
2. patients are more involved in the planning of their care.

The major issue would seem to be that the care plans must be readily available to all those who need them whether it be nurses to carry out care or patients to know what care has been planned. If they are at the patient's bedside because that makes them more usable, then confidentiality must be taken into account. However if for any reason they are kept elsewhere they must be in a place where they can be used. It has been known for patients to sleep with them under their pillows!

When the nursing care plan has been developed the implementation phase begins. 'Implementing is the initiation and completion of actions necessary to accomplish the defined goals' (Yura and Walsh, 1988). The actions may be carried out by the nurse who wrote the plan but they may well be carried out by a number of other people as well, such as the patient himself, his relatives or friends, or by any other member of the nursing team providing the actions they take are appropriate to their role and competence.

During the course of carrying out the prescribed actions new problems may arise. The nurse must use her knowledge and experience to decide what significance they may have and whether they should necessitate the modification of the plan. She will also be testing out whether the planned interventions are indeed enabling the patient to reach the stated outcomes. Giving care provides the nurse with a sense of satisfaction and fulfilment of her role while making it possible for her to give value and dignity to the patient.

The success of the implementation phase depends on the quality of the written plan of care but the measurement of that success depends on the care with which the evaluation is carried out.

References

Benner, P. (1984) *From Novice to Expert, excellence and power in clinical nursing practice*. Addison-Wesley, California.

Carnevali, D. (1983) *Nursing Care Planning: Diagnosis and Management*, 3rd edn. J.B. Lippincott, Philadelphia.

Department of Health (1991) *The Patient's Charter*. HMSO, London.

Department of Health (1992) Letter from the Chief Nursing Officer, 29 July. Richmond House, London.

Sundeen, S.J., Stuart, G.W.,Rankin, E.A.D. and Cohen, S. (1989) *Nurse–Client Interaction*, 4th edn. C.V. Mosby, St Louis.

United Kingdom Central Council (1992) *Code of Professional Conduct*, 3rd edn. UKCC, London.

Wilkinson, F. (1989) Care plan location – does it really matter? *Nursing Standard*, **3**, 35–7.

Wright, S. (1990) Patients' access to nursing records. *Nursing Standard*, **5**, 21–4.

Yura, H. and Walsh, M.B. (1988) *The Nursing Process*, 5th edn. Appleton-Century-Crofts, Norwalk.

7

Evaluation

Evaluation is that part of the cycle of the nursing process when we judge the effectiveness or otherwise of nursing action towards goal achievements. Evaluation means 'to determine the value of something' (*Chambers English Dictionary*, 1980). It is at times a complex process calling for an analysis of information that we perceive with our senses and its interpretation is based on experience, knowledge and our value system.

Fortunately, the goal setting approach to care used today, with its measurable criteria, should make evaluation easier than in the past. When taking a broad perspective of evaluation it is a help to keep in mind Donabedian's (1969) triad of structure, process and outcome, which was developed to aid the evaluation of medical care, illustrated in Figure 7.1.

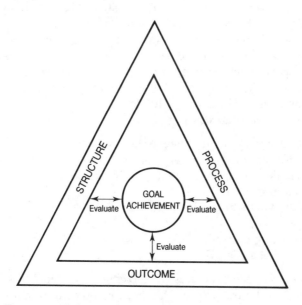

Fig. 7.1. Framework for evaluating goal setting achievement (based on Donabedian, 1969)

Structure is concerned with the evaluation of the conditions under which care and service are provided, e.g. the buildings, equipment, staff, time available and management style.

Process is when the evaluator looks at what the health carer does to and for the patient, and how.

Outcome is the result of the care on the patient.

The triad is a useful framework to keep in mind when analysing progress towards the goal achievement itself, for we can ask ourselves:

1.   were the resources adequate? (structure)
2.   how did the nurse carry out the care? (process) and
3.   what effect did it have on the patient? (outcome)

Evaluation is often thought of as the last stage in the nursing process. This is not always so, for we are evaluating the effectiveness of care from the time care begins. For example, we judge how well a patient responds when he gets out of bed for the first time after an operation or how well a wound is healing and how competent a new mother is in bathing her baby. This is known as *formative* evaluation, which is sometimes written on a review date. *Summative* evaluation is made when the goal, or the sum of the goals, is achieved or care is discontinued. This is when the total plan of care should be evaluated; thus evaluation statements can be seen as a record of the consequences of care.

All evaluation statements should be written, dated and signed by the person making the evaluation. Ideally this should be the nurse who has set the goals with the patient and/or has had the responsibility for his care, for she should have the most knowledge about the patient. Indeed, there may be occasions when the patient may write down his own evaluation. His responses will enable a more effective and realistic evaluation to be carried out. Photographs and drawings may sometimes be used as a record of progress and thus of evaluation.

The evaluation procedure is as follows:

1.   Check goal statement on review or target date.
2.   Collect information – table might be useful as a source of reference.
3.   Consult patient and, if necessary, significant others.
4.   Make a judgement.
5.   Evaluation will include one of the following:
     a) goal achieved
     b) goal no longer relevant
     c) goal not yet achieved.

If the result is 'goal achieved' it is wise to check if the goal was pertinent to the problem and if the problem has been resolved or modified to such an extent that no further progress is required or possible. 'Goal no longer relevant' may mean that the patient's condition has changed to such an extent that he no longer can or even needs to reach the goal because the problem has changed or ceased to exist. 'Goal not achieved' may mean that the time for evaluation was unrealistic or that the patient's condition has changed, making the resolution of the problem slower than anticipated. When analysing the reason for this it would be useful to check if the problem is still the same or if the nursing action was correct.

In checking problem definition, consider the following:

1. Does the patient still have the problem?
2. Is the problem clearly stated with descriptions that enable a measurement to take place when necessary and that there is no area for misinterpretation, as this could lead to inappropriate goal setting? For example:
   - Poor mobility
   - Anxious
   - Spits at people
   - Large varicose ulcer
3. Does the patient acknowledge or understand his problem?
4. Has the patient been told about his problem?

Table 7.1 Aids to evaluation

Records	Observation	Communications	Measurement
Reports	Look	Talking	Measuring utensils for fluids
Care plans	Touch	Listening	Watch
Notes	Listen	Touching	Thermometer
Flow charts	Smell	Observing	
Graphs		Non-verbal clues	Sphygmo manometer
Scales		Empathy	Scales
Photographs			Ruler
Drawings			Chemical analysis
			Graphs
			Camera

In respect of analysis of prescribed nursing action as written in the care plan, consider the following:

1. Are the instructions clearly stated?
2. Are the instructions realistic for the patient and the resources available?
3. Are the instructions still applicable for this particular problem?
4. Have any changes in the care been noted and at the right time?
5. Are the instructions being followed; if not, why not? It is wise to

check previous evaluation statements and progress notes, also check with colleagues if there is any doubt whether written instructions are being followed.

6. Are all the people mentioned in the instructions involved; if not, why not?
7. Is the equipment available to enable care to be carried out?
8. Are the actions based on outmoded practices and therefore inappropriate and hindering goal achievement?
9. Does the patient know what is expected of him? If he does not, this too may hinder goal achievement.

It is sensible when analysing prescribed nursing actions to check if the frequency of goal review and resultant changes in any prescription have been noted in the action column.

Finally, if the goal, problem and action have been checked and everything seems correct, please 'relook' at the goal statement for there is probably a need to reset the time limits.

In Module 5 of *Systematic Approach to Nursing Care* (Open University, 1984) it is pointed out that goals that remain static can be a positive sign when applied to potential problems, for it is a sign of success if the situation does not change. This can mean that the patient's condition is improving and/or that the preventative and checking measures are being effective in preventing the occurrence of the potential problem.

How to measure

It has been noted earlier that all goal statements must have criteria. There are times when a physical measurement can be used, which makes evaluation of the effectiveness of care much easier and more precise. In order to effect this measurement different 'tools' may be used. Sometimes these tools may be instruments designed specifically for the purpose:

- Jugs and graduated measuring utensils for fluid
- Watch for timing pulse and respiration
- Thermometer to measure temperature
- Sphygmomanometer to measure blood pressure
- Scales to measure weight
- Tape measure/ruler to measure distance
- Reagent strip for chemical analysis
- Charts and graphs to measure frequency and demonstrate clinical observations
- Camera for photographs of posture, wounds, etc.

Measuring cards using sterile material to assess changes in the size of pressure sores may also be designed.

One method of dealing with a record of changing frequencies, for example when measuring bowel actions, wound drainage, vomiting, convulsions, etc., might be to represent them by use of a bar chart or histogram. For example, if a goal was related to the reduction in the number of convulsions a patient was having, progress towards the goal might be recorded on a chart such as that shown in Figure 7.2. The nurse would be able to fill in one section of the chart when each convulsion was observed, giving a total at the end of 24 hours or whenever was appropriate.

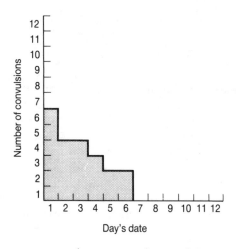

Fig. 7.2.   Chart to measure frequency of convulsions

Graphic illustration is also useful in indicating recorded changes in temperature, blood pressure, pattern of incontinence or sleep patterns. In this case a linear representation is used.

Where subjective information is in the goal statement, as when the patient reports a feeling, a thought or reacts to something, it is sometimes possible also to use a 'tool' which makes evaluation easier; scales which monitor, for example, pain, anxiety and mood. Points on these scales are agreed by discussion with the patient. They are then used to indicate the effectiveness of the care and in so doing the progress towards the stated goal. It is a wise investment to search for such tools that have been validated by use and in research, for example the Glasgow Coma Scale as shown in McFarlane and Castledine (1982). Actual measurements will be set in agreement with the patient and using his words.

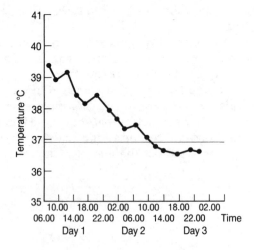

Fig. 7.3.   Graph to demonstrate clinical observations

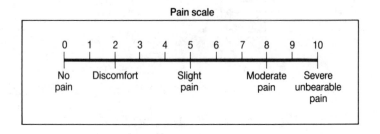

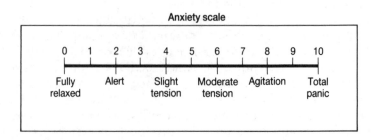

Fig. 7.4.   Evaluation scale

Writing the evaluation statement

As previously indicated, the evaluation statement will refer to the patient's actual status in relation to the goal on the target or review date.

It is also evident that a statement may need to be made outside the planned dates if anything unusual happens to the patient. A written statement will be noted in the evaluation column on the care plan, progress notes or medical notes, whichever is the choice of the organisation. The problem definition, the goal statement and the nursing prescription (action column) should be reviewed and changed if necessary.

What to write

If the goal has been achieved the statement can read – 'goal achieved'. However, a short statement saying *what* the goal achieved gives a clearer picture of the result of care, for example, 'drank 3 litres of fluid in 24 hours' or 'gained 4 kg in weight'.

Remember to date and sign the evaluation statement.

If the goal has not been achieved but remains relevant, perhaps because progress is slower than anticipated, it is necessary to write a short evaluation statement and set a new review or target date. At times, particularly with goal steps, a statement referring to the criteria within the goal is all that is necessary, such as: 'Sat in chair without discomfort whilst Anne prepared the seed bed – joking about her crooked rows "like a dog's hind leg" '.

When you consider what the patient's problem was you can see that he became less withdrawn and responded to his surroundings.

Evaluation statements may at times also mention such things as changes in care but not in any detail, as this will go in the nursing prescription (action) column.

Many nurses cross through the problem, goal and the nursing prescription when the goal is achieved or the problem ceases to exist. However, the nursing record is classified as a primary document and 'it will form a permanent part of the patient's case folder together with other documents'. Amongst other things it is 'a source of information about the patient. It is an aid to teaching and research. It can be used for legal purposes' (King's Fund Centre, 1979). The primary document is stored for many years after the last date of entry. It therefore follows that the information on the nursing record should be available, accurate and legible. Information should not be erased; if it is crossed through, use a thin ink line, enabling the words underneath to be seen. The procedure to be followed should be dictated by the health authority, NHS unit or trust.

Accountability

Whereas all levels of nurses may provide information that will enable evaluation to take place, it is the named nurse who should make the final judgement about the success or otherwise towards goal achievement.

References

Chambers English Century Dictionary (1980) MacDonald, A.M. (ed.). W.R. Chambers Ltd, Edinburgh.

Donabedian, A. (1969) Some issues in evaluating the quality of nursing care *American Journal of Public Health*, **59**, 1833–6.

King's Fund Centre (1979) *A Handbook for Nurse to Nurse report*. King's Fund Centre, London.

McFarlane, Baroness of Llandaff and Castledine G (1982) *A Guide to the Practice of Nursing using the Nursing Process*, CV Mosby Co., London.

Open University (1984) *Systematic Approach to Nursing Care – An Introduction*. Open University Learning/Teaching Package, Module 5. Open University Press, Milton Keynes.

8

The framework for quality

The purpose of this chapter is to give the reader an overview of the changes occurring in the National Health Service at the beginning of the 1990s in relation to the quality of patient care. We also feel it will be helpful to define and comment on some of the many terms that refer to quality initiatives these days. This will be followed by a discussion on total quality management and quality assurance.

Changes in the national health service

The White Paper *Working for Patients* (DoH, 1989) set out plans to reform and strengthen the NHS. It stated its simple aim as, 'Being a service that puts patients first'. Cynics might have wondered what carers had been doing prior to this pronouncement!

Following the White Paper, the NHS and Community Care Act 1990 brought further changes in the management of the Health Service. Many individual units became directly managed, but remained answerable to the district health authority. Some units opted for National Health Service trust status with their own executive body. They opted out of local control and are answerable to the Secretary of State.

The greatest change, however, was the introduction of a business ethic. District health authorities became purchasing authorities and their role included: identifying the health needs of the community; the provision of services to meet these needs; developing quality assurance and evaluation systems. Thus, the purchasing authority achieves its objectives 'by the negotiation of contracts for services, specified by cost, quality and volume.' (Roy, 1990).

The directly managed units and NHS trusts provide services which are subject to contracts with purchasers. These must be established in order to secure sufficient income to cover some of the expenditure incurred in providing health care. They are expected to offer a quality service and value for money set out within a detailed business plan, which tells the purchaser what can be provided to meet the requirements. A quality assurance plan is also included in the business plan.

Many units and trusts have set up clinical directorates to encourage the delegation of budgets and resource allocation to patient care level. The directorates are seen as a means of giving greater autonomy of action to those people clinically involved in the day to day management of patient care. (Some hospitals had been using such systems from the middle of the 1980s.)

Generally speaking, it is a doctor who has the role of manager of the clinical directorate. For the first time professionals are having to take on a role which requires business skills. The advent of clinical directorates has also meant that the traditional management structures and professional hierarchies have disappeared, with nothing initially to replace the support that such systems provided. This is something that could hinder quality initiatives; however the people who work together implementing such systems could provide mutual support. The effects of change which brought about the business ethos, together with the implementation of systems to evaluate performance, can be threatening and cause stress to individuals. If nurses are to give a quality service it behoves them to do what they can to lessen the adverse effects of change, for themselves and for colleagues.

Discussion of the terms used for quality initiatives

There is much debate about whether it is possible to define quality. What is important is to spend time considering the concept and how it fits in with the values of the organisation, the community, professional groups and individuals. Such activity enables a mission statement to be made about the intention of the organisation (see below). However, this activity may also identify some areas of dissension which will have to be addressed. It can also prove an educational experience where people share ideas from different perspectives and thus hopefully learn from each other. A definition of quality will act as a guideline for staff, patient and the community. *Chambers English Dictionary* (1980) defines quality as: 'that which makes a thing what it is: nature: character: kind: property: attribute: grade of goodness: excellence'. Van Maanen (1979) writes, 'Quality is a concept hard to define, it embodies an abstract . . . Quality is a concept that expresses reality, but at the same time expresses aspects of desirability'. She points out that it is not easy to make a clear distinction between the real and the ideal.

Accreditation

The recognition by certification that an organisation has reached an acceptable level of performance. In the United Kingdom accreditation is used by educational institutions to award certificate degrees and diplomas. A distinction should be drawn between academic accreditation and the accreditation which follows monitoring in the Health Service. The NHS Management Executive (1993a) defines accreditation as, 'a system of external and independent audit. It uses preset and agreed standards and measures performance and achievement against these standards to show where further improvements can be made'. The Management Executive also point out that there are a number of different accreditation models being used. They include, 'the Kings Fund organisational audit which is specifically designed to assist the management of health care facilities to assess, evaluate and develop their services'.

> Clinical audit is a cooperative, multiprofessional assessment of the efficacy, social acceptability and economic efficiency of the care and treatment of patients with specified diseases, disorders or disabilities. The focus can be the process or outcome of the individual components of care or the total care experience.'
>
> (Barnett and Kemp, (1994)

Audit is a term much used today with many interpretations, these will be discussed in more detail in Chapter 11.

Evaluate

'To determine the value' (*Chambers English Dictionary*, 1980). Evaluation is making judgements; it occurs when monitoring is carried out. Evaluation is a complex activity and has many interpretations, depending on the context in which it is being applied. Evaluation should be as objective as is humanly possible.

Mission statement

This is a statement of the purpose of the organisation, based on the values and beliefs of its members. below is an example of such a statement:

SOUTHAMPTON UNIVERSITY HOSPITALS TRUST

MISSION STATEMENT

SOUTHAMPTON UNIVERSITY HOSPITALS TRUST
PROMOTES, PROTECTS AND IMPROVES HEALTH THROUGH

PERFORMANCE – PROVIDING EFFECTIVE TREATMENT AND
CARE FOR PATIENTS THROUGH OUR EXTENSIVE RANGE OF
GENERAL AND SPECIALIST SERVICES

DEVELOPMENT – PROVIDING TEACHING AND
PROFESSIONAL TRAINING, AND MAINTAINING OUR FIRM
COMMITMENT TO RESEARCH, INNOVATION AND STAFF
DEVELOPMENT

QUALITY – PURSUING EXCELLENCE IN EVERYTHING WE DO

Monitoring

Checking something or someone for a specific purposes. Jones *et al.*
(1981) state, 'Monitoring is usually thought of as measuring performance
against agreed standards and objectives and taking any necessary action
when the standards are not met' cited by Kemp (1983). The frequency
of monitoring activities depends on the needs of the organisation in
which it is occurring. It is influenced by what is to be monitored and
why. Informal monitoring can occur as one walks around care areas.
However, formal monitoring must be planned and those carrying out
the exercise must have received education and training to enable them
to do the job effectively.

Peer review

A procedure used by people of equal qualification and grade to assess the
performance of their peers; for example, medical audit where clinicians
evaluate the work of their colleagues. It may also be carried out by a
specific committee or a group of two or three people. The purpose can
be to give an objective assessment of the quality of performance of an
individual, guided by standards and indicators. It may also be used to
judge an individual's eligibility for promotion.

Quality circle

A group of people from the same work area, who meet together to
identify and solve work related problems guided by a laid down protocol.

The group do not measure care as such, although the aim is quality improvement. Some of the work can highlight areas that need standard setting.

Quality control

A system of checking resources and activities against predetermined specification or standards in an attempt to ensure they are achieved. An example is daily checks of the emergency equipment to ensure equipment and drugs are available, in working order and safe.

Quality improvement

A philosophical concept or it can refer to a system to improve quality. For example, the directorate staff may identify some area giving them concern, such as complaints about the temperature of the food. The staff then set targets and/or standards to enable the problem to be resolved and thus the quality to be improved. Quality improvement is a continuous process.

Quality monitoring methodology

A method that is used to measure, assess or evaluate quality. This includes monitoring procedure, the instrument or indicator, correlating and presenting the results. Such a system may be developed locally, bought or leased from the owners or use an already established methodology.

Total quality management (TQM)

This may be defined as:

> An approach to improve the effectiveness and flexibility of business as a whole. It is essentially a way of organising and involving the whole organisation; every department, every activity, each part of it must work properly together, recognising that every person and every activity affects, and in turn is affected by others.
>
> (Oakland, 1989)

The NHS Management Executive (1993b) state:

In a mature TQM organisation:
- everything is driven by the customers' needs;
- a highly trained and motivated workforce continually seeks better ways of working;
- change is based on measured fact and monitored in a continuous cycle of improvement;

- errors are relentlessly traced and eliminated;
- a hands-on management drives the search for quality.

Thus it can be seen that TQM aims to bring all aspects of quality together and involve all levels of staff with each one having a direct or indirect effect on the service and the performance of each other. Whilst this seems right, it is very complex given the actual number and variety of staff, their individual working philosophies and professional demands. The needs of the various client groups, resources available and the expectation of the society in which we live – all these factors must be considered. At the very heart of this activity is the need for the quality of the service being provided to be right for the patient and the community and that it is fairly allocated within the confines of the resources available.

The directorate staff must play their part in making TQM a reality. They need to be well informed and vigilant, to develop the confidence to put forward ideas to improve care and performance and to constructively critique any innovation being implemented. Most staff are concerned to do their best – they want to be effective and give safe care. However they will require educational facilities to enable them to cope with innovations and to grow professionally. They must want to be successful in the 'market place'. They need to know about the business plan and, as far as their directorate or department is concerned, to have made a contribution towards its development. The directorate must be able to give the quality service they are offering, it must not just be a 'paper exercise'. The staff need to have a commitment towards quality care and performance.

We have said that health care changes are focusing on providing a quality service with the needs of the patient paramount. Let us not forget to listen to what they or their advocates are saying; included in this group are the community health councils (CHC) and consumer groups who look after the welfare of patients and carers. Such groups could and do take part in evaluating care; for example, many CHCs carry out consumer surveys in outpatients departments. Many patient support groups have set their own standards; for example, the National Association for the Welfare of Children in Hospital, now known as Action for Sick Children, whose aim it is to integrate good practice in all areas where children are given care, not only in hospitals. The directorates should actively encourage patient participation in evaluating care.

TQM requires a big outlay for education and training. It also needs some support mechanism and a central person or group to oversee the activities. Most organisations do have a director of quality and a steering group. Nurses should use this resource when needed.

In TQM the concept of quality . . . is referred to as a process. Quality is described as a journey rather than a destination. '. . . high quality is assured by promoting the efforts of well-intentioned employees as a cycle of never ending improvement'. (Norman and Redfern, 1993).

Quality should not be a separate issue, it should permeate all health care activities. It should encompass not just the technical but also the caring skills which all good professionals use.

Quality assurance programme

'Comprises the means and methods to assess the effectiveness and efficiency of health care delivery and the instrument and activities to overcome recognised deficiencies' (WHO, 1986). To this definition we would add, 'and to reinforce good practice'.

Whilst total quality management involves the whole unit or trust, a quality assurance programme can be unit or trust managed or specific to a directorate or a department, such as physiotherapy or catering. It is part of TQM. The purpose of the quality assurance programme is to set up and maintain quality initiatives which will enable staff to develop standards or indicators of quality, monitor and evaluate the service being provided and take action on the findings.

In organising and developing a quality assurance programme there is a need to set up a steering group to advise and coordinate all quality activities. The steering group members write a statement of purpose, set objectives and ensure the consultative process is gone through. A quality monitoring methodology can be designed to suit the needs of the group intending to use it or it may be bought in or an already established methodology can be modified to suit local needs. (Measuring system will be discussed later.) Such a methodology also guides monitoring, evaluation and calibration of the results. Auditors are chosen and given the appropriate education and training. The results are normally sent to the director of quality and to the manager of the area being monitored.

All staff whose work is to be monitored must be given information about what is expected of them; they and their managers must have an appreciation of change theory to enable them to cope with the consequences of having their work monitored. The staff who develop audit protocols and standards must also have the appropriate educational help.

We have discussed some of the organisational changes that are occurring at this time. The word *organisation* means, 'to give orderly structure to, frame and put into working order, make arrangements for or initiate' (*Concise Oxford Dictionary*, 1982). We must be careful that our orderly structure does not take over from our desire to acknowledge and maintain the patients' uniqueness and individuality.

References

Barnett D, E, Kemp N (1984) in press The A to Z of Applied Quality for Clinical Managers in Hospital. Chapman and Hall. London.

Chambers English Dictionary (1980) MacDonald, M.A. (ed.). Edinburgh.

Concise Oxford Dictionary (1982) Sykes, J.B. (ed.), Oxford University Press, Oxford.

Department of Health (1989). Working for Patients. HMSO, London.

Hill, F.M. and Taylor, W.A. (1991). *International Journal of Educational Management,* **5,** 4–9.

Jones, D., Crossley–Holland, C. and Matus, T. (1981) *The Role of the Nursing Officer.* DHSS, London.

Kemp N. (1983) Monitoring the Nursing Process. *Nursing Focus.* July/August. 4. Issue 8. 1–2.

National Health Service and Community Care Act 1990. HMSO, London.

NHS Management Executive (1993a). Quality Roadshow. You make the Difference. Department of Health, London, p. 10.

NHS Management Executive (1993b). *The Quality Journey. A Guide to Total Quality Management in the NHS.* NHS Management Executive, Leeds, p. 20.

Norman, I. and Redfern, S. (1993). The Quality of Nursing. *Nursing Times,* **89,** No. 27, 40–43.

Oakland, J.S. (1989) *Total Quality Management.* Heinemann, Oxford.

Roy, S. (1990) The White Paper and nursing. *Nursing Standard,* **4,** 17–19.

Van Maanen, J.M. (1979) Perspectives and problems on quality of nursing care: an overview of contributions from North America and recent developments in Europe. *Journal of Advanced Nursing.* **4,** 377–89.

World Health Organisation (1986) European Newsletter on Quality Assurance, Vol. 3, No 4. WHO, Utrecht.

9

Quality versus cost – the nursing paradox

It is becoming increasingly obvious that nursing is being called to account for the cost of what it does. Earlier in this book we described the change which has taken place in the ethos of the National Health Service so that its operation is now firmly placed in a business culture with health care services being in the market place. Purchasers are looking for value for money in identifying the service they wish to purchase for their clients. That service may be to provide a percentage reduction in the number of patients on the waiting list for hip replacements or hernia repairs. It is equally important that the care received by clients requiring such surgery is of good quality. An integral part of any NHS contract is the standards written into the agreement.

This chapter sets out to examine the costs of nursing care. Consideration is given to staffing issues and the very real problem of ensuring that skill mix is not just cost effective but that there is no compromise in the delivery of quality care. The cost of nursing includes both the product and procedure by which it is delivered. Research is used to illustrate some of the ways in which nurses could improve this aspect of their practice. A major part of the chapter then goes on to discuss means by which nurses may more precisely identify and cost the process of nursing. It enters the debate about nursing diagnosis and argues that if used wisely this can provide an effective tool for nurses,to ensure that the work they do is clearly identified in terms of patient costs.

However, we never lose sight of the need to ensure that in considering cost it is always equated with quality. To quote Sharon Roberts(1990), 'Nurses must agree among themselves that nursing diagnoses represent the way to achieve quality patient care'. It does this by providing and organising a commonly accepted structure for the creation of nursing practice standards.

Nurses are the most numerous and collectively the most expensive group of staff in the NHS (Bond, 1991). Managers looking for ways to cut costs are undoudtedly going to explore this fact. Already there have been numerous investigations both locally and nationally to review skill mix, sometimes resulting in the loss of jobs for qualified nurses and their replacement with other less qualified, and possibly less expensive, staff. Evidence for this comes both from the Bevan Report on the management and utilisation of operating theatres (1990) and the work of the National Audit Office (1991) on outpatient services. These reports have caused great concern amongst nurses. This concern has perhaps been allevi-ated to a degree by two more recent reports, discussed in the next para-graph,indicating that fewer does not mean better.

It has to be said that the notion that less qualified staff are necessarily less expensive does not readily stand up to testing. A study by Gray and Smail (1982) cited in Gibbs *et al.* (1991) found that an examination of a threefold increase in the number of unqualified nurses in Scottish hospi-tals over the period 1950 to 1979 indicated that related savings were less than 5% in the total pay bill. There is, however, no indication as to the effects on the quality of care which was provided for patients during this period. Nurses must clearly guard against managers making decisions which are based on cost alone and do not consider cost-effectiveness. The profession must be able to give clear evidence of the quality and nature of the work it does. It must be constantly watchful that it does not abrogate its responsibility to assess, plan and give care and to evaluate its effectiveness by allowing others to have this role.

In June 1992 the North Western RHA produced a skill mix report which suggested that 'Qualified nurses provide better, cost-effective standards of care' (O'Byrne, 1992). This report was the result of a two year study using a quality pointer tool which helps nurses to assess what happens on a ward when the level of care falls. Eight medical and surgical wards from a number of north-western hospitals were used and various skill mix strategies were tried in order to measure their impact on the standard of care. It was possible to measure the relationship between the reduction in the wage bill and the lowering of care standards.

Earlier in 1991 the Department of Health's own study on grade mix was published. The result of this work reported by Daloni Carlisle in the *Nursing Times* indicates that 'investment in a highly qualified, well-trained nursing workforce leads to good quality patient care'. Although the report was unable to give accurate guidance on skill mix numbers and grades, it did show that 'increasing the qualifications of the nurses gives better quality of care'. It is interesting that the *Nursing Times*, reporting the publication of the report, includes a response from a DoH spokesman who is quoted as saying, 'Decisions on appropriate skill mix rest with local managers'. This is a sentiment echoed by Hibbs (1992) in her article on 'Skill mix in hospital', when she states that 'When management invests in the staff they are on their way to providing the quality of care we all wish to achieve' for it is also true that, 'Poor care is expensive, increasing hospital stays, treating complications and legal costs'. The question then arises of how the nurse can ensure managers take account of such reports.

Some interesting research reports from the USA substantiate these findings. Work done by Hartz *et al.* (1989), cited in Aiken and Fagin (1992), shows that 'hospitals with a high proportion of registered nurses provide a better quality of care, as measured by lower mortality rates'. An analysis by Fagin of current literature in the USA on cost-effectiveness of nursing care suggests that, 'data are accumulating to attest to the powerful contribution nurses are making to enhancing the quality of care, promoting health and lowering total system costs'. Her conclusion is based on considering work done with:

1. nursing in hospitals, including nurse/doctor relationships;
2. the use of nurse practitioners which are similar to British clinical nurse specialists and;
3. alternative modes of care, particularly in community and elderly nursing care.

As mentioned earlier, primary nursing is increasingly advocated in this country as a preferred method of organising nursing care. Anecdotal evidence and the decreasing number of American studies on this subject suggest a falling away of interest, at least in the USA. An analysis by Diers in Aiken and Fagin (1992) suggests that there is 'a sizable body of literature supporting the view that primary nursing is worth trying, that its implementation is a worthwhile experience for both patients and nurses and that the outcomes may be significantly better than that for other forms of nursing organisation'. Unfortunately there is little real evidence that primary nursing is cost-effective. Experienced managers do however, find that it is at least as cost-effective as more traditional methods and suggest that this may be because in this country nurses are more realistic and practical in their approach to its implementation.

Many professionals would argue that primary nursing allows the nurse to be giving more 'hands-on' care and this underlines the importance of nursing and the role of the nurse. There is no doubt that nurses must control nursing but many nurses have a problem with what elements of caring can safely be delegated to people other than nurses. Herein lies part of the dilemma. Nursing can be described in lists of tasks people do, activities and behaviours which can be separately identified and hence costed as items but in the words of June Clark in the introduction to the RCN's publication *The Value of Nursing* (1992), 'The special quality of nursing and nurses is the ability to blend knowledge, skill, experience and empathy into seemingly effort-less clinical practice'.

A difficulty also arises in terms of the nurse reconciling her role as practitioner with that of resource manager. It means that individual nurses must not leave such considerations only to those who have traditionally been part of management but must each be orientated to consider their actions in terms of cost and value. Safety and quality must never be compromised for the sake of savings as what may be seen as savings in the short term may very well end up as a long term problem, costing the service much more in the end.

Karen Ballard's paper in Dunne (1991) discusses the elements of caring which staff need to consider in ensuring that 'efficiency and cost effectiveness are not put above quality of care'. Perhaps the first essential is to raise staff awareness of the way in which poor planning can lead to waste, both of time and energy.

In the context of the ward careful thought must be given to the cost of equipment which is constantly in use and to the consideration of new items which may be suggested. Not only should resources be our concern but so also should the procedures which we use. Although there has been increasing use of research in changing practice, so that nursing is now based more on fact than on ritual, we have still some considerable way to go in this respect.

It is interesting in this context to note the work done in the ICU of St Peter's Hospital, Chertsey, and reported by Ballard in Dunne (1991). The staff of this unit set out to identify the cost of patient care, initially in considering the cost of items of equipment; however this led to a consideration of the procedures used. They soon became aware that by avoiding unnecessary waste caused by poor planning which might affect both patient comfort and wear and tear on equipment they were also improving the quality of the care they were giving.

Increasingly, also, nursing is using more technology in practice. There is as yet little research on the effect of this increase on the quality and cost of care. This is an area which requires future consideration. A study reported by Jacox in Aiken and Fagin (1991) looks at the cost implications of using heparinised as distinct from normal saline flushes for intravenous devices. It was found that it took 45–60 seconds to perform the normal saline flush as opposed to 120–160 seconds for the heparinised flush. There was no reported significant difference in the rates of phlebitis, clotting or infiltration rates between the two methods but 12.9 per cent of those flushed with heparinised saline leaked and had to be restarted. The consequent savings to the health service of using normal saline flushes was estimated at $30–40 000 a year. Patients also obviously benefited from the decreased problem of leakage. Clearly there is a need for increasing research in this area and this is a very strong incentive to prevent research and development monies being cut in times of economic stringencies.

Nurses at ward level are increasingly involved in budgeting. In terms of resources that means that they are required to make decisions which may have far reaching implications for patient care in relation to the purchasing of equipment. It is essential that they are in a position to make judgements based on adequate evaluation and assessment of the products they are recommending for purchase. This calls for accurate and up-to-date information on products. Nurses must make sure that the product information they are using is objectively assessed and has a research basis. They must be careful not to be swayed by the persuasive language of glossy advertising or slick marketing techniques.

It is acknowledged that it is indeed difficult in a busy ward or department always to stand back and make decisions which are thought through logically and coolly. Nurses in the present NHS ethos of business driven activity need to develop a more critical approach to their decision making. Neither must they be persuaded on the basis of cost alone but must constantly keep value and quality as their watchwords.

So far we have concentrated on the rather more easily measurable aspects of nursing work, but we must also consider other activities which nurses do which are based on an identification of perceived nursing need or health care deficits. These are the items identified on nursing care plans as actual or potential nursing problems. A cursory glance at these on any ward will highlight certain difficulties in categorising identified items so that they could be used as indicators of the need for nursing intervention, in the way that a medical diagnosis may determine the possible line of medical or surgical treatment. This creates some difficulties in the communication of nursing activity between professionals but, more importantly in the context of the present discussion, makes it extremely difficult to handle units of nursing information in a way which lends itself readily to the identification of cost.

In this country and for considerably longer in the USA, consideration has been given to the need to identify the cost of medical care. This led to the development of DRGs (diagnostic related groups). 'DRGs were developed to define the mix of cases treated in hospitals so that comparisons for cost and quality could be made among institutions or services'. (Diers in Aitken and Fagin, 1991). It should always be remembered in this debate that it is not merely the efficiency of the use of resources which is under consideration but also its effectiveness in terms of the quality of care provided.

Patients are allocated to a DRG dependent on their principal diagnosis (the chief reason for their admission) although other key factors in the determination of cost are the secondary conditions identified at the time and the principal procedure for treatment related to the principal diagnosis. The cost of the patient's hospital care is then determined by his DRG classification. This takes account of the predicted length of stay, the number of services provided and the intensity of these services. This work was done initially to identify costs of inpatient care and does not take account of outpatient, accident and emergency or home care, all of which are major items of expenditure in any health care system. Further work in these areas is being done on both sides of the Atlantic. Work in the UK has also extended beyond using DRGs to include considering 'cost per case' and 'case mix systems'. Whatever the system, it is acknowledged that there is a need to analyse and thence itemise elements of the process of health care, in order to effectively manage health budgets.

It can be seen that this description has not directly made reference to nursing care which is an essential element in the process of patient care. Clearly there must be a way of categorising nursing which allows for its accurate costing and which is easily identified by all nurses, thus allowing for better communication and more rational debate at a time when the value of nursing and the work of the qualified nurse is being questioned. Such decisions about nursing are not easy, what nurses do is highly complex and decision making must be done with clear thinking and a considerable degree of intellectual skill.

> Nursing must be able to name itself and to describe what it does in order to function effectively in a world where computerised information is used to establish everything from diagnosis related groups to cardiac output. Until nurses can name what they do and assign a computer code to that name, we may be neither reimbursed nor recognised as a profession with unique skills and knowledge.
>
> (*Classification Systems for Describing Nursing Practice*, 1989, p. 3, cited in Aitken and Fagin, 1991)

One way of doing this is to return to the concept of nursing diagnosis and consider this alongside that of medical diagnosis. There was considerable resistance to the introduction of this concept when it was first advocated in the 1970s, at the time when the movement towards the introduction of the nursing process was advancing in this country. It was important at that time to establish the need to identify nursing separately from medicine and the word 'diagnosis' had a strict medical connotation to it. Perhaps a better interprofessional awareness will have reduced this problem and it may be apposite to return to the concept now recognising that it aids us to be more accurate in our description of what we are about. In terms of cost the use of nursing diagnosis points to the need to consider factors other than medical condition or surgical procedure in calculating resource consumption.

The word *diagnosis* may have medical connotations in the eyes of nurses but it is a word not exclusive to health care and we do have garages which offer diagnostic facilities for the ills of our cars and plumbers who may diagnose deficiencies in our drains. Yura and Walsh, in their book *The Nursing Process*, review the development of nursing diagnosis and the ways in which it has been defined. One way of describing it is as the end process of assessment. It is 'an expression of the status of the client, identifying assets and strengths as well as disturbances and weaknesses'.

The legal profession in the USA is beginning to recognise nursing diagnosis within the definition of nursing. This is particularly well stated by Bernzweig (cited in Yura and Walsh, 1988), a member of the New York Bar, when she says:

> . . . nursing diagnosis is an established and independent function of the professional nurse and calls for the utmost in intelligent judgement and sensitivity on her part . . . Good nursing diagnosis is one of the keys to the successful practice of nursing and is therefore a skill all nurses should learn.

However, there is still considerable debate amongst our colleagues on the other side of the Atlantic about this concept. In the June 1991 edition of the *Journal of Emergency Nursing* there are two guest editorials clearly setting out the opposing views. Jill Curry finds the language of nursing diagnosis 'pompous, if not downright silly'. She feels that it is an 'esoteric exercise' which 'has alienated nurses from one another' and exhorts nurses to 'abstain from designing secret, obscure, elitist codes' and 'arm ourselves with a language in which we can truly think and maintain our professional being'.

Her opponent, Eleanore Kirsch, offers an alternative view. Her concept of nursing diagnosis is that 'it is one way to help nurses describe, *share* and demonstrate their contributions to health care'. She acknowledges that there are difficulties with language, but feels that one reason is that the origins of the diagnosis movement emerged from a medical model. She emphasises the importance of sharing knowledge to improve patient care and to enable nurses to refocus on independent nursing practice. This ability of nursing diagnosis to allow nurses to *share* their thinking about nursing is echoed by Roberts (1990). In an article focusing on achieving professional autonomy she suggests that:

> Such a framework can bring all professional groups together around a common focal point, provide a vehicle for standardising patient care, and raise the status of nurses' professional role among other professions.'

In a rather philosophical article Gail Mitchell (1991) argues that by using nursing diagnosis nurses may create an ethical problem inasmuch as the nurse may 'do the patient harm' by judging and labelling them in such a way as to cause the patient to feel 'misunderstood, disconnected and alone'. In establishing herself as an expert she 'automatically delegates the other person to a lower less valued status'. In accepting that the patient's perception of the value of health must be acknowledged the nurse denies the importance of the knowledge and understanding she has as a professional person and the ability she may have to improve the quality of the patient's life. Mitchell accepts that nursing diagnosis may be helpful in dealing with biophysical problems but denies its use in those of a psychosocial nature.

Seifert and Grandusky (1990), writing in the *AORN Journal*, do not have this difficulty. They assert that it is not possible to divorce the biophysical from the psychosocial in the assessment of the patient's problems and state: 'A more holistic approach that incorporates psychological and social aspects of the patient's experience will facilitate the identification of nursing diagnoses'.

The dilemma rests in the need to recognise that which is nursing and to identify the unique contribution which nurses give to patient care. In order to do this a language has to be developed which can easily be shared both within and between professions. At the same time this language must not lose the uniqueness of the individual and his personal response both in biophysical and psychosocial terms to the health care problem which besets him. It is possible that within the diagnostic statement there is room for both. A consideration of nursing diagnosis in practice will perhaps give clarity.

With reference back to page 40, there is a problem described as:

Problem: As a newly diagnosed diabetic, lacks the skill to test urine.

In terms of nursing diagnosis this would be described as:

Nursing diagnosis: Knowledge deficit related to recently diagnosed diabetes; cannot test urine.

This indicates the components of the diagnostic statement, which are:

1. *Human response or problem*: This identifies an actual or potential problem which can be affected by nursing care, i.e. knowledge deficit.
2. *Related factors*: These may precede, contribute to or simply be associated with the human response. They enable the diagnosis to fit the individual patient, i.e. recently diagnosed diabetes.
3. *Signs and symptoms:* These are the defining characteristics which are drawn from the assessment data. There may be several so only the most relevant should be included, i.e. cannot test urine.

Yura and Walsh (1988) include guidelines for writing the nursing diagnosis. These are:

1. Keep the process simple.
2. Cite problems that the nurse can do something about.
3. Make clear and concise statements of problems and diagnoses.
4. Describe the aetiology clearly and concisely.
5. Differentiate the problem and the aetiology clearly.
6. Use the diagnostic statement as the basis for the next step in client care.

The Clinical Skillbuilders publication on *Better Documentation* (1992) includes some of the pitfalls which nurses must avoid when writing nursing diagnoses:

1. Use nursing diagnoses not medical diagnoses or interventions.
2. Use all relevant assessment data.
3. Take enough time to analyse the assessment data.
4. Interpret the assessment data accurately.
5. Keep data up to date.

The major work in this field in the USA has been undertaken by the North American Nursing Diagnosis Association (NANDA) which was set up in 1983. Their published definition is:

> A clinical judgement about individual, family or community responses to actual and potential health problems/life processes. Nursing diagnoses provide the basis for selection of nursing interventions to achieve outcomes for which the nurse is accountable.
>
> (Kim *et al*. 1991)

NANDA has subsequently published a taxonomy which is the most widely accepted classification system of nursing diagnosis although there are many others, often related to particular models of nursing. The categories which they use are the areas of psychosocial human functioning and physiological regulation, such as:

- Beliefs/decision making
- Comfort
- Physical integrity
- Elimination
- Feeling.

In the category of physical integrity comes elements such as 'impaired skin integrity while under feeling comes 'anxiety, hopelessness etc.'.

'Nursing diagnoses can guide the direction of health care delivery by costing out services' (Roberts, 1990). Using nursing diagnoses as a means of identifying cost is not without difficulty, however, as nursing diagnoses are multiple and vary throughout the patient's stay or during the period when nursing interventions are needed. Medical diagnosis is more constant although complications may occur to add to the initial diagnosis. Diers in Aiken and Fagin (1992) suggests that nursing diagnoses may be weighted to take account of the fact that, for the nurse, some are more important than others or more time consuming, e.g. the diabetic patient's knowledge deficit would be of greater importance than that of someone who had just had a hernia repair. Where medical diagnosis forms the basis on which costing of care is determined then using nursing diagnosis is much more likely to indicate the need for extensions to intended length of stay in hospital or to the need for care services in the community. An interesting idea of Halloran (1985) cited by Diers in Aiken and Fagin (1991) is that of using medical diagnosis as a weight to nursing diagnosis, which may be worthy of further research.

Further work by Halloran cited in Roberts (1990) indicates that 'variations in nursing work load were better explained by the patient's nursing condition than the patient's medical condition'. Patient nursing conditions were measured by the number and types of nursing diagnosis. This seems a fairly obvious assertion but it is good to find it backed up by research. In the same article, work by Skydell and Arndt describes the comparative cost of nursing care related to DRG 243 as ranged from $510.40 to $1 051.60, a difference of 106 per cent. The cost of nursing care was calculated by assessing nursing work load through the number of hours required each day of stay for patients with the same DRG.

In the same way as nursing diagnosis gives us the ability to be more precise in our description of the need for nursing care, so must we strive for precision in our statements of nursing interventions. One of the principles of quality is doing the job right first time, rather than going back to correct errors. We must also consider whether that which we have described as nursing interventions are actually carried out by trained or untrained staff. Even if we believe that nursing diagnosis is the way to categorise nursing need we must also also have means of costing the way that the need is met.

Stilwell and Hawley (1993), of the Health Services Research Unit, have described 'a methodology for attributing labour costs to individual patients'. Their method involved dividing nursing labour into 3 categories:

1. direct labour
2. indirect labour
3. other labour.

where 'direct labour' included all face-to-face care, e.g. hygiene, vital signs, 'indirect labour' included writing reports and care plans and 'other labour' might include anything from 'housekeeping to private study'.

They used observation as the method of obtaining their data and, following analysis, were able to attribute the categories described to a variety of grades of staff. Direct costs were attributed to individual patients. These account only for one third of total labour costs so that it was necessary to establish a consistent method of allocating both indirect and other costs. Indirect costs were allocated to patients in proportion to direct costs, on the basis that those patients who required a high proportion of direct care would need 'a relatively large amount of indirect time'. The costs of other labour were then divided equally amongst all the patients. This study was able to demonstrate 'considerable differences between the nursing costs of patients on the same ward and on different wards'.

This allocation of time may be open to question. The relatively independent patient may require considerable indirect care in terms of discharge planning, for example.

It is interesting to note that patient costs on the gynaecology ward used in the survey were significantly higher than those on the other medical and surgical wards. Trained staff ratios on this ward were 82 per cent compared with 30 per cent on the medical ward and an average of 50 per cent overall. The proportion of direct care given to patients on this ward was also less. However, it is not possible to say whether there was any difference in the quality of care provided on any ward, nor in the patient satisfaction levels. Somehow, as nurses, we need to bring this work on costing of care together with the need to maintain quality by employing the right proportion of qualified nurses to be cost-effective and to satisfy the consumer . . . a tall order indeed.

Brooks (1992) quotes a recent issue of a US magazine entitled *Modern Health Care* where the quality of nursing care is described as the number one factor in determining patient satisfaction. 'Hospitals use the quality of their nursing care as the major element of their advertising campaigns'. She goes on to point out that the value society attributes to people is most often measured by their remuneration. In this case it could be said that nursing is a bargain! It is important that nurses continue to work towards a more measurable way of identifying what they do. They must be able to substantiate the cost-effectiveness of their caring because if they do not there are others who would do it for them.

References

Aiken, L.H. and Fagin, C.M. (1992) *Charting Nursing's Future.* J.B. Lippincott, Philadelphia.

Better Documentation (1992) Advisory Board. Clinical Skills Builders, Sprinhouse Corporation, Pennsylvania, USA.

Bevan, P.G. (1990) *The Management and Utilisation of Operating Theatres*, Committee Report. NHS Management Executive, London.

Bond, S. (1991) Input to outcome. *Nursing Times*, **87**, 25–7.

Brooks, A.M. (1992) The cost of care: an American experience. *Nursing Standard*, **6**(45), 32–6.

Carlisle, D. (1992) Care improves with qualified workers. *Nursing Times*, **88**(42), 6.

Curry, J. (1991) Nursing diagnosis: Communication impaired. *Journal of Emergency Nursing*, **17**(3), 124.

Diers, D. (1992) Diagnosis Related Groups and the Measurement of Nursing. In *Charting Nursing's Future*, Aiken and Fagin (eds). J.B. Lippincotte.

Dunne, L. (ed) (1991) *How Many Nurses Do I Need?* Wolfe Publishing Ltd, London.

Fagin (1992). Cost Effectiveness of Nursing Care Revisited: 1981–1990. In *Charting Nursing's Future*, Aitken and Fagin (eds). J.B. Lippincotte.

Gibbs, I., McCaughan, D., Griffiths, M. (1991) Skill mix in nursing: a selective review of the literature. *Journal of Advanced Nursing*, **16**, 242–9.

Hibbs, P.J. (1992) Skill mix in hospital. *Senior Nurse*, **12**(5), 14–17.

Kim, M.J., McFarland, G.K., McLane, A.M. (1991) *Pocket Guide to Nursing Diagnoses*, 4th edn. C.V. Mosby, St Louis.

Kirsch, E. (1991) Treating nursing's response to nursing diagnosis. *Journal of Emergency Nursing*, **17**(3), 125–6.

Mitchell, G.J. (1991) Nursing diagnosis: an ethical analysis image. *Journal of Nursing Scholarship*, **23**(2), 99–103.

National Audit Office (1991) *NHS Outpatient Services*, HMSO, London.

O'Byrne, J. (1992) Does fewer mean better? *Nursing Standard*. **6**(39), 20–1.

Roberts, S.L. (1990) Achieving professional autonomy through nursing diagnosis and nursing DRGs. *Nursing Administration Quarterly*, **Summer**, 54–60.

Royal College of Nursing (1992) *The Value of Nursing*. RCN, London.

Seifert, P.C. and Grandusky, R.J. (1990) Nursing diagnoses: their use in developing care plans. *AORN Journal* **51**(4), 1008–21.

Stilwell, J.A. and Hawley, C.A. (1993) The costs of nursing care. *Journal of Nursing Management*, **1**, 25–30.

Yura, H. and Walsh, M.B. (1988) *The Nursing Process*, 5th edn. Appleton-Century-Crofts, Norwalk.

10

Setting standards for nursing care

In this chapter we focus on how to set standards that relate to patient care. Through the generosity of colleagues we have included standards which they have developed, to illustrate some of the current work taking place in different specialities. We discuss the reasons and describe a variety of approaches to standard setting in use at this time. It is our belief that no one approach is necessarily right for all groups setting patient care standards. We end the chapter with suggestions on how to validate standards and criteria together with a discussion on measurement.

Before setting standards it is worth reminding ourselves of the principles set out in the RCN's first report *Standards of Nursing Care* in 1979, reaffirmed in 1981. Those principles are still relevant today.

a) Nurses, as individuals, develop their own standards of care. It is for the profession as a whole to agree on acceptable levels of excellence.

b) Good nursing is planned, systematic and focused on goals mutually agreed with the patient, where possible and appropriate. This implies a continuous pattern of assessment, planning, action and review.

c) Agreed standards of care provide a baseline for measurement.

d) Standards of care will influence not only nursing practice but also nursing education, nursing management and nursing research. While every nurse has a responsibility for setting and maintaining standards, the roles of the nurse practitioner, educator and manager will be different.

The word *standard* is used in everyday language. Most nurses strive to maintain a good standard of care, but do not necessarily know how to set and measure such standards to prove the quality of what they do.

The reasons for setting standards can be considered in relation to the following:

The patient

The patient has a right to the best possible care. Standard setting can go some way to meet the patient's concerns and requirements particularly if their views are listened to and then incorporated into standards.

The professional

As professionals we are accountable to society for our practice. The trained nurse, midwife and health visitor is regulated by the *Code of Professional Conduct* issued by the UKCC (1992). This is the body which is responsible for the standards of the profession's conduct and is invested with this power by statute. Standards represent the expected quality of nursing for society, colleagues and the practitioners themselves. They enable practice to be evaluated, reviewed and when needed, changed. Standards also enable comparisons to be made between clinical areas. They empower nurses to objectively evaluate their practice.

Society

Setting and measuring standards and taking any necessary action on the findings is a way of assuring society of the quality of the profession's practice.

Expansion of knowledge

Professional knowledge will be increased and enhanced by examining practice, considering new concepts and procedures, reinforcing that which is good and changing that which is not. By the same token such activity can aid nursing research by testing concepts and providing information obtained at evaluation. Research findings may also be used to help set standards.

The law

People are generally now more aware of their rights and these have been reinforced under the Patient's Charter (DoH, 1991). The Ombudsman's report (Reid, 1992) shows that more patients than ever are complaining about the poor practice of nurses and other health carers. Therefore, as Tingle (1992) states, 'The existence of standards of care could well go to the credit of the hospital in a court case by showing that there is a controlled environment of care'. However, it is to be hoped that having standards in place will only be to the credit of the hospital if the standards have been used to evaluate care and there is proof that action was taken to correct low scores. 'It takes courage and persistence to use the usual hospital complaints process. Value everyone that gets through as a golden opportunity to find out more' (Barnett and Kemp, 1994). Focusing on the subjects of complaints can highlight areas in which to set standards. This in turn should improve practice and decrease the number of complaints, thereby reducing the stress of those who complain and staff whose work is subject to investigation. It should also decrease the amount of money paid out in litigation.

Politics and management

In chapter 8 we discussed the political reasons for being involved in quality assurance activities and the influence this has had on the management of health care. The government requires professionals in the NHS to evaluate the service given to patients, which means that staff are more clearly answerable for what they do. We must not forget that managers are also answerable and accountable, at the highest level, to the Secretary of State. There have always been rules and regulations regarding the way a person works, however, with increased accountability there will be increased monitoring of that work. Tingle (1992) pointed out:

> If a nurse consistently and without good reason, fails to follow and achieve reasonable realistic and agreed standards of care, he/she could face employment disciplinary proceedings. Reasonable standards of care do not create a higher duty to act, they clarify existing duties in the contract of employment.

Personal values

Good nurses want to improve their practice and most have a desire to help people. They care about individuals. Standard setting enables nurses to translate their values into workable standards, benefiting not only the patient but other carers as well. The process will also enable good ideas about care to be shared. Standard setting is not easy, it can cause stress amongst those trying to produce the standard by which they and others will be judged. However, if the standard setting is well organised and the standards used correctly, morale should be maintained and enhanced.

Multidisciplinary approach

Standard setting could encourage collaboration between the different caring professions. One of the difficulties of evaluating care is that it is not always possible to say who is really responsible for the results – after all, care is not usually the work of one professional group. As account-ability in respect of quality scores becomes clear the need for collaboration will become more apparent and urgent.

Resources

Outmoded and inefficient procedures will be identified and changed and more relevant, appropriate and efficient ones implemented, thereby improving the service to the patient and using resources more effec-tively.

Having given some reasons for standard setting we now go on to discuss the subject in more detail. There are many definitions and we include two:

> A standard is an explicit statement of conditions to be fulfilled.
>
> (WHO, 1981)

> A standard is a professionally agreed level of performance appropriate to the population addressed, which is observable, achievable, measurable and desirable.
>
> (RCN, 1986)

Example of a standard:

> All adult patients have a named nurse responsible for their nursing care during their stay on the high dependency unit.

Criteria (singular *criterion*) enables a standard to be measured; they are detailed indicators of the standard and can be specific to the area or type of patient. (RCN, 1986).

Example of one of the criteria for the above standard:

> The patient can state that his/her nursing care was discussed and planned by his/her named nurse.
>
> (South Birmingham Health Authority (Acute Unit)
> Royal Orthopaedic Hospital. High Dependency Unit)

Standards should be:

- **Clearly stated**, unambiguous, leaving no room for doubt
- **Desirable** and achievable, enhancing good care and improving poor care
- **Acceptable** to the population they are meant for, not offending cultural, ethnic or professional values
- **Realistic**, meaning they are practical and can be achieved
- **Measurable**, phrased in such a way that they enable a judgement to be made as to whether the standard has or is being achieved.

Some standards statements can stand alone because they contain the measurement. Below is a standard that does contain a measurement and could be evaluated as it is. However the addition of criteria enables more information to be obtained as they are more specific. A score may be assigned to the judgement made about standards and/or criteria.

The details at the beginning of the standard (see p. 88) are based on the RCN DySSSy model and will be discussed later, as will the Structure, process and outcome approach.

Standards should be subject to regular evaluation and revision to ensure they remain valid and reliable; an annual review is reasonable.

One of the characteristics of a standard which may give problems is the term *realistic*. If we are not careful those desirable things that patients and carers should have will not be addressed because of scarce resources. However, if the patient has a right to the service (as defined by the government, the profession, the objectives of the provider or purchasing authority together with the philosophy of the ward/s or department) and it seems reasonable, then set the standard. The process of ratifying the standard may highlight the difficulties and as a consequence bring forth the necessary resources or a compromise. However, any compromise must not be at the expense of patient safety or professional integrity. The standards must be reasonable because, of course, we all have a duty to use resources wisely.

Standards should also be set by people with knowledge and experience of the subject to be evaluated and of the policies, procedures and resources available in the unit or trust. Much has been said about ownership, meaning that the people who set the standards own them. It follows that if nurses have developed standards for their own area they are more likely to use them, accept the results and be prepared to look

Standard and criteria developed by staff and patients of the Oaks Ward of Ashworth Special Hospital under the direction of Tom Catterall, Manager

Standard reference number	OAK/001	Implementation date: 05.8.93.
Topic	Social skills	Review standard by: 08.8.94.
Subtopic	Group discussions	Signature of DNS:
Care group	Rehabilitation	Signature of SCHM:
		Date: 30.7.93.

Standard statement: Each Saturday evening a group of 4–6 patients meet to discuss topics taken from the week's daily newspapers.

Criteria:

Structure	Process	Outcome
3 members of staff.	During the week each member of the group collects two news items and place them in the collection point.	The current affairs discussion group meet every Saturday.
Comfortable available room.		A group discussion takes place.
Collection of weekly newspapers	The group meets on Saturday evening and a topic of conversation is selected out of the collection point envelope.	A record is made in each patient's clinical notes that they have attended the current affairs discussion group.
A collection point for topics.	Staff members using their communication skills then facilitate a group discussion on the topic chosen.	
Refreshments	A member of staff records all patients' attendance in their current clinical notes.	

positively for ways to improve low scores. The standards will also be specific to the area in which they will be used and there should be a feeling of pride in the work. But remember the old adage about 'reinventing the wheel'. Standard setting is not easy, it takes a long time and a lot of intellectual effort and can be costly. Consider if it would be better to see what has already been developed in an area of the same speciality and ask permission to modify the standards to the local needs. If permission is obtained the source of the standards must be acknowledged. Despite the difficulties in setting standards there are, as we have said, advantages in developing local standards. Nonetheless, if managers want staff to set standards and be committed to a system, they have to provide education, positive support and the resources to carry out the exercise and staff have to be given the right to constructively comment on the work.

Another area of debate in the setting of standards relates to the 'top down, bottom up' approach. The first may appear as an edict from the mangers to the clinical staff. Too often in the past systems of working, including quality monitoring methodologies, were imposed by managers with little or no prior consultation with clinical staff nor an appreciation of the stresses such action created. Two obvious results are resistance to change and a lack of commitment to the innovation. The bottom-up approach 'involves participation by the immediate care givers and recipients of care in the planning and evaluation of the service they receive' (Garvey and Manley, 1992). The latter concept also means that ideas which come from the clinical staff are considered by the manager and if thought to be feasible are implemented and the source of the idea acknowledged. The manager may also suggest a project and allow the clinical staff to develop the work, thus enhancing a sense of ownership and encouraging good working relationships. An effective manager should make some contribution to the standard setting because, as we have said, staff have to be given support and the necessary resources and acknowledgement for the work carried out. It will also increases the manager's credibility with staff to do so.

'Standards derive from two sources: empirical . . . derive from actual practice . . . normative from a body of legitimate knowledge and values (Donabedian, 1966). The latter means from research findings, text books, professional publications, policies, procedures, professional guidelines, rules and regulations. Empirical and normative material can at times cause conflict and ethical problems. For instance, is it right to set standards based on theoretical concepts and or research findings which aim for the highest care, but which the staff may not be able to reach through lack of training, ability, understanding and resources? The material may also be in conflict with the unit's or trust's philosophy or be unreasonable for the patient group. Conversely, should nurses set standards based on procedures which, although seeming to be effective in practice, have not been evaluated? Patricia Benner (1984) asserts that, 'Perceptual awareness is central to good nursing judgement and it begins with vague hunches'. She also says, 'Expert nurses know that in all cases definitive evaluation of a patient's condition requires more than vague hunches, but through their experience they have learned to allow their perception to lead to confirming evidence'. This confirming evidence could be established by setting and evaluating the standards based on empirical sources. Similarly, standards based on normative material could also validate whether the practice is right for the care area.

Not all standards that relate to nursing focus directly on the patient, but are set to ensure nursing care is of high quality thus benefiting the patient, for instance:

Standards (3 of 5) Relating to the Nurse at Trust Board Level.
1.   The nurse at board level provides leadership and professional nursing advice on the development of nursing practice in the Trust.
2.   The nurse at board level provides a specialist nursing contribution for the board in an advisory capacity.
3.   The nurse at board level provides the professional leadership and expertise to heighten the focus on professional nursing within the corporate strategic direction of the Trust.

(Pamella Leggett. Portsmouth Hospitals NHS Trust 1993)

Regional Standard for Nursing Services – Standard 9.
Managers of nursing services ensure that the system for allocation of nurses is designed to meet individual patients' needs for nursing care, commensurate with each nurse's qualifications, skills and experience.

Criterion (one of nine)
All nurses, including those employed through an agency, are professionally qualified for the posts to which they are appointed and are currently registered with the UKCC.

(Wessex Regional Health Authority 1989)

Criteria are statements or questions which relate specifically to the standard, enabling it to be measured. They are the responses one would expect if the standard has been or is being achieved, for example the presence of the correct resources, or information, the right environment, the desired action of a carer and the planned outcome for the patient, planned with him whenever possible. Below is a further example of a standard with criteria which are specific and relevant to the standard

Standard statement: All patients are provided with a quiet environment suitable to facilitate rest and sleep.

Criteria:

Structure	Process	Outcome
All nurses are aware of the importance of quietness of speech and working practices.	Nurses carry out care quietly.	Patients' sleep is not disturbed by nurses' conversation.
Fixtures and fittings are properly maintained to work quietly.	Nurses wear quiet shoes.	Patients' sleep is not disturbed by avoidable noise.

Medical Unit, Selly Oak Hospital, Birmingham

The above standard will be referred to in Chapter 11.

It is sensible to be consistent in the way criteria are expressed. Do not use a mixture of questions and statements for the same standard. If criteria are statements they should be phrased to indicate that something either applies or does not apply, which allows either a yes or no response to which can be added a numerical weight.

Criteria should be:

- **Clinically** sound, written by staff who are up-to-date in the relevant clinical practice and who know about the unit policies;
- **Professionally acceptable** – not contravening accepted professional values and beliefs;
- **Specific** – one clear statement or question about the desired result pertaining to the environment, performance or outcome.
- **Achievable** and realistic, given the resources and ability of staff;
- **Capable of measurement**, written in such a way as to enable a check to be made that something is or is not available. has been carried out or not, has been achieved or not. The result is capable of having a score assigned to it;
- **Free of bias**: 'Each patient to whom a criterion is applied should have an equal opportunity to obtain a good score' (Zimmer, 1974);
- **Valid**, which refers to the extent to which a criterion actually measures what it is supposed to measure. For example, when setting standards about a patient receiving a low fat diet you would not expect to see a criterion that related to the meals being served on time;
- **Reliable**, which refers to the ability of the criterion or an instrument to consistently provide an accurate measurement whenever

it is used, provided it is used for the purpose intended. For example, criteria designed to measure the exercise tolerance of the young cardiac patient may not be reliable in measuring the exercise tolerance of the elderly cardiac patient.

Each criterion should focus on only one thing to be measured, otherwise the scoring may be difficult or impossible. For example, in a standard about discharge planning, one would not write that a patient demonstrates the use of a walking frame and a hoist, because this would require two responses and if they were different a problem over scoring would arise.

The criteria can be evaluated against actual practice by one or a combination of the following methods:

- Checking patient care nursing records
- Interviewing patients, relatives, and or staff
- Direct observation of patient care, nursing practice and management
- Checking the ward /department environment
- Checking the provision of support services.

It is our observation that many criteria are written in the future tense, for example, 'the patient will', 'the nurse will', 'equipment will be'. How can one measure something that 'will' when it has not yet occurred? Similarly the word 'should' is also overused. How is this to be measured? We may agree that something should happen but unless it has happened or is happening we cannot measure it.

To measure quality we need an instrument which we see as' being composed of both standards and criteria, in a format that guides evaluation and enables a score of quality to be obtained' (Kemp and Richardson, 1990). It can be as simple as a checklist that requires a yes or no response. The evaluation may be carried out by one or a combination of the methods mentioned above.

However, quality information can also be obtained by conducting patient surveys, by sending out questionnaires or by an audit committee examining patient care records. The information from the last two will be retrospective. The survey results can be a combination of retrospective and current information. Normally the quality measuring instrument used in the patient care area produces current data. It is up to individual groups to choose the best way to gather the information they need.

Approaches to standard setting

As we may use a model or conceptual framework of nursing to help plan nursing care, so we can use a model or list to guide our standard setting and criteria development. Avedis Donabedian's (1966) approach to evaluating care suggests that three headings could be used:

Structure describes the factors in the organisation that enable care to be carried out. These are resources such as equipment, the condition of the environment, the right number and mix of staff, rules and regulations, policies and procedures and conditions of service.

Process describes the performance of the carer and, at times, the patient. This can include: assessing the patient's needs, planning and carrying out care with the patient or significant others, setting and evaluating goals, discharge planning, teaching and counselling the patient, effective communication and documenting information correctly.

Outcome describes the desired results of care. It can include the patient's health status, his behaviour, opinions and level of knowledge and skill.

Standards can be written without reference to the Donabedian approach or written in one of the domains of structure, process or outcome – it depends on what is to be measured. Similarly, criteria may or may not be based in one or all of the three domains. It is what is required to measure the standard that matters.

Many of the early quality instruments used to measure nursing care were based on process. Today there is a move to focus on outcomes. This is worrying for nursing, because it is just as important to measure what the nurse does as it is to measure outcome. Consider: a patient may recover from a stroke and on being discharged walk out of the ward unaided. But what about the care he received? Are we sure he got the messages his family sent him? Was his pyjama jacket changed when it was soiled? Did the nurse always include him in the conversations when care was given? Did anyone notice he was frightened and do something about it? We must be vigilant and ensure patients' nursing needs are being met and that is why we must not only focus on outcomes. It is not enough to advocate that process be measured if outcomes are not met. That behaviour will ultimately lower the standards of nursing, which we may not know about until we receive complaints from dissatisfied patients. Patients' care may have been delayed or compromised and patients made miserable although the end results were good. The ends do not justify the means in such cases.

Example of a process standard:
All patients are treated in a courteous manner.

Data source	Criteria	Yes	No
	Care staff call the patient by the name the patient has chosen.		
Ask patient	*Do the nurses call you by the name you prefer?*		
Observe nurses giving bedside care and report:	The patient is included in conversation that takes place at his/her bedside.		
	Does the nurse tell the patient what is happening?		
	Staff introduce themselves to patients when they meet for the first time.		
Ask patient:	*If a new nurse comes to help you does she/he tell you her/his name?*		

Many people find Maxwell's (1984) dimensions of health care quality a useful guide to setting standards. There are six dimensions:

1. Access to service
2. Relevance to need (for the whole community)
3. Effectiveness (for individual)
4. Equity (fairness)
5. Social acceptability
6. Efficiency and economy.

Below is an example of a standard based on one such dimension:

West Dorset Community Health NHS Trust

Core Standards

| *Focus:* | Nurse | – | qualified |
| | | – | unqualified |

Specialties: Medicine
Surgery
Elderly Care/Rehabilitation
Community
Theatre
Outpatient department
Casualty

Date written:
Quality dimension: Effectiveness (Practice)
Standard statement: All nurses within West Dorset Community Health
NHS Trust provide an effective service.

	Criteria	**Yes**	**No**
1.	All nurses are clinically competent within their speciality, monitored by: a) clinical standards of care (6 monthly) b) clinical audit c) observation		
2.	All nurses fulfil the objectives within their job descriptions and individual performance review		
3.	All nurses implement national, regional and local directives by: a) Patient's Charter (national and local) b) regional standards c) local standards		

Comments for negative measurement:

National, regional and local requirement:
UKCC Professional Codes of Conduct
Job description
Local standards
Local clinical audit
Patient's Charter – national and local
Miles M and Hemer P (1993)

(The standards are based on Maxwell's (1984) dimensions of health care).

'The criteria written against the above standard statement serves as the measurement tool, and is currently monitored once every six months' (Miles, 1993).

Some nurses set standards according to their area of responsibility, for example:

Educational standard:
All English National Board Clinical Studies Courses have a management committee to monitor the course, which meets at least twice a year.

Criteria	Yes	No
1. Is there a list of management committee members?		
2. Has the committee met at least twice a year?		
3. Has the course been monitored?		
4. Is there evidence of how the course has been monitored?		
5. Is there evidence which reflects the outcomes of those suggestions made by the committee?		

Barbara Milburn, Southampton University College of Nursing and Midwifery

Yet another approach to standard setting is used by Excelcare which is 'a microcomputer based system for planning, documenting, staffing, evaluating and costing nursing service based on nursing standards' (Price Waterhouse, 1987). The standards are set locally but follow the framework developed by Elizabeth Mason and Judith Daugherty. The system is based on the nursing process and uses 'units of care' which Mason (1984) defines as, 'the cluster of process, outcome and content standards that define the nursing care for a given nurse diagnosis, health problem, or need; a desirable point on the health–illness continuum; or a specific development stage', which are individualised for each patient. The outcome standards are used for evaluation. On command, checklists can be produced which can be used to measure compliance with standards. This is a system where individual patients do benefit directly from the evaluation of the standards, which is not usual with many other systems. We will refer to Excelcare in the next Chapter. Below is an example of a patient's care plan which uses the Excelcare approach.

Supplementary Care Plan/Documentation

Weymouth & District Hospital

Maud Alexander Ward

Patient* Date of birth Age Sex Speciality

Nursing focus in Admission.

Statement: The patient is admitted to the ward and is made to feel welcome. The patient is orientated to the ward environment and their needs are identified and care planned to meet these needs

1. Prepare bed area and equipment before patient's arrival.
2. Greet patient, introduce self and patients in the area, and allow time for expression of anxieties.
3. Give explanation and information for ward orientation.
4. Arrange for valuable property to be deposited in a safe place.
5. Check and attach identity band to the patient.
6. Complete nursing data base.
7. Plan care according to identified needs.

Named nurse/team leader:

Associate named nurse/team leader:

Sharon Waight, West Dorset Hospital

*The patient's details have been removed from this care plan. The outcome part of this care plan will be shown in the next chapter.

The RCN Standard Setting Programme under the leadership of Alison Kitson has developed the Dynamic Standard Setting System (DySSSy) based on the original work by Helen Kendall and the nurses of West Berkshire Health Authority.

> The dynamic standard setting system involves groups of ward staff setting, monitoring and evaluating their own practice. It takes a problem solving approach, where topics for quality improvement are identified by the group, criteria formulated, a standard statement agreed, and measurement techniques determined. The final part of the cycle involves the group in agreeing appropriate courses of action which are subsequently evaluated in light of the agreed standards
>
> (Kitson, 1988).

'DySSSy is a "bottom up" problem-based approach to quality assurance involving the monitoring and evaluation of standards of care by practitioners'. (RCN, 1990).

The system encourages ownership of the standards and also wisely involves the manager, who is expected to sign the standard's form to show she or he is aware of and approves the standard. Work is in progress to develop a software package for DySSSy. The framework of the standard form contains a topic, subtopic and care section (shown on the standard on page 88). The topic is a means of identifying the broad category for the standard, the subtopic is more specific and the care group is the particular group of patients the standard is meant to address. The format in which the criteria are presented to the user with the structure, process and outcome criteria alongside each other, is sometimes difficult to read and requires a separate audit form which gives extra work. If the criteria were listed one under the other with a column for scoring at the side there would be no need to develop a separate audit sheet; although there would in some cases be a need to include instructions for the person carrying out the audit. Some of the standards shown in this chapter have successfully used the DySSSy approach and we show an audit form for one of those standards in the next chapter.

Below is an example of standard with structure, process and outcome criteria in a format which is used as an audit tool:

Andover District Community Health Care NHS Trust
and Andover Social Services

Images Statement for District Nursing (Health) and
Home Carers (Social Services)

Statement: The district nurse and home carer promote a professional/competent image at all times

Structure	Evaluation Yes	Evaluation No	Comments
1. The district nurse has an identity card			
2. Policies and procedures or guidelines are available.			
Process			
1. All staff introduce herself/himself to patients/carers/clients.			
2. All staff acknowledge that he/she is a guest in the patient's/client's home.			
3. All staff understand the rule of confidentiality.			
Outcomes			
1. The patient/client/carer states: a) that staff introduced themselves b) staff look clean and tidy c) staff were invited into their home and respected their equipment/property.			
2. The district nurse is able to show an up to date PIN No.			

Mary Critcher, Andover War Memorial Community Hospital

Preparation for setting standards and developing criteria

An open meeting should be held at the start of the project to set standards, to tell staff what is proposed. It will also give people the chance to air their views and to contribute to the project. If patients are going to be asked questions the ethics committee should be consulted, although the unit or trust quality assurance group may have some agreement with the ethics committee so that individual groups do not have to approach them.

As has been pointed out, standard setting is not easy and can cause stress. Many nurses feel that they should know how to set standards, particularly those that relate to their area of work. They should be reassured that it is accepted that they may feel anxious. They should be reminded that whilst not all nurses have the skill to set standards, most will know what constitutes good care. Everyone setting standards for the first time requires positive support which includes education and time.

The person arranging the above meeting and giving the support and resources will be the manager or senior nurse. She will take on the role of coordinator because she has access to resources and the authority to bring about change. Her normal role includes monitoring the activities within her area of responsibility, therefore her experience and knowledge will be valuable. She may contribute to the standard setting as an equal in the group or she may choose not to attend all meetings, preferring perhaps to leave the members to get on with the work.

We suggest that the person coordinating the project should:

1. **Set up a standard setting group**, ensuring the members are representative of the nursing staff, including a teacher. It is our experience that six people is a comfortable number to work with; ideally the same people should carry out the work to give continuity.
2. **Choose a group leader and a facilitator.** The group leader must be clinically credible and be able to organise and lead the group activities. She should be able to create an atmosphere that enables the group members to share ideas and critically analyse what they produce without ridicule or unfair criticism, whilst at the same time acknowledging good work.

   The facilitator requires knowledge about standard setting and some skills in teaching. Her role is to assist the group leader, to guide, support and provide education when necessary. The facilitator may not have an indepth knowledge of standard setting, so ask the unit or trust quality assurance group for help. Failing this, ask the education department staff if they can recommend anyone to help.

3. **Check what resources are available**, including administrative help. Choose a venue that is comfortable to work in and away from the phone. Obtain information about what is happing locally and in the region. Many regions now have a quality assurance network. Libraries are always a good source of information, as are the professional colleges.

The coodinator, together with the group leader and facilitator, will then:

1. clarify the responsibility and authority of the group members and its relationship with the unit's or trust's quality assurance group;
2. Carry out a literature search and obtain or compile a short glossary of terms;
3. Devise simple guidelines to help members set standards;
4. Set objectives, short and long term. This enables the group to check progress at specific times. Standards and criteria can take time;
5. Specify the frequency and length of time the group will work. The group may meet once a month (in work time) for one to two hours. The group members will need time to show the work to their colleagues and to relay the suggestions back to the working group. It is our experience that two hours is long enough to spend carrying out such work. Whilst such activity can be stimulating it is also very taxing intellectually.
6. Provide education for the group. If possible the group should attend a workshop on group dynamics. However, if this is not possible the leader and the facilitator should have an appreciation of the problems that can occur when people work together in a group – particularly when attempting to produce innovatory work. Everyone should be given instruction on how to set standards and criteria.

The standard setting group work begins

Examine the unit's or trust's mission statement and the wards' philosophy. Discuss their relevance to the work of the group and how it will affect standard setting. This part of the process should not be ignored because it helps the members to sort out their ideas about quality. Occasionally such a discussion may uncover some uncomfortable facts about a member's attitude to patients, which the leader has to handle carefully.

Choose the subject/s to be evaluated. The standards may be set to apply to all the patients in the ward or people who have a particular diagnosis or syndrome or of the same age category, gender or culture. Standards may be set because something is giving concern, such as poor communications, high infection rates or the findings from complaints. There may be a need to evaluate new procedures or old. Consider the recent research findings relevant to the subject/s to be evaluated. Examine new ideas. It may be pertinent to consult the findings from recent patient surveys and the work of relevant patient support groups. It can be demoralising to focus just on areas of suspected weakness as staff have a right to have good care acknowledged, as well as acknowledging the need to improve poor care.

Within this book we have talked about the rights of patients to be involved in their care. Ideally a person representing patients should be on a standard setting group. This may not be realistic but the next best thing is to ask patients for their ideas about what constitutes good care by way of patient satisfaction surveys or interviews. It has been observed that what patients value highly are not necessarily given the same priority by nurses. Some examples of what a group of patients on a surgical ward said makes good care were: 'nurses smiling', 'receiving phone messages', 'being included in conversations', 'doctors sitting and listening properly', 'comfortable chairs', 'soundproofed lavatories', 'being given up-to-date information', having smelly dressings changed frequently', 'bells answered promptly', 'nurses speaking clearly at bedside', 'hot food' (Kemp, 1985). As professionals we should know about care and safe practice, but we should never forget to ask ourselves what the patient would want if he were setting the standard or the criterion and ideally we should ask him.

Select a model or list to guide the standard setting. It is very easy to get distracted when setting standards, so draw up the model or list the topics for which standards have to be set. Have it available each time the group meets, because it will serve as a reminder of what the group is supposed to be doing.

Decide the approach and the framework in which the standards will be used, how they will be monitored and the method of measurement. It is realistic to do this before setting the standards because it can affect the way nurses think about the standards, the style in which they are written and the way they are set out. These decisions will in some cases influence the way the criteria are worded and whether instructions are required for auditors. It may also require extra work to produce a separate auditing tool.

Setting the standards

The number of standards to write will depend on the subject/s to be evaluated and the objectives of the group. If using a daily living activities list, one standard per need may be enough. However, a model may call for three standards or more for each part of the model. It is appreciated that different groups may choose their own method of setting standards but we have found the following helpful:

Choose the subject for a standard (guided by the model or list). Ask the following questions and discuss the answers:

- Is the subject chosen for the standard in the nurse's sphere of influence?
- What is the purpose of the standard?
- Will the standard improve care?
- What should be in the standard?
- Is it realistic to set the standard?
- Will the standard apply fairly to the population or the group it is meant for?

When agreement is reached to set the standard, each member writes the standard as clearly and succinctly as possible. The wording will tell people what the patient has the right to expect. Together the members critique the standards, assessing whether the standards appears:

- Unambiguous
- Desirable
- Acceptable
- Realistic
- Measurable.

When the standards have been discussed the best is chosen and further work to refine it is carried out.

Developing the criteria

Keep in mind the approach being used for the instrument and ask the following questions:

- What is needed to carry out care?
- Who would give the care?
- What does the carer do?
- What would the patient want to happen?
- What performance is expected from the patient?
- What do the nurses or carers want to happen as a result of care?
- What would have happened if the patient's goals are being achieved?

- How many criteria per standard?

Together 'brainstorm' criteria to measure the standard, noting each one down on a chart. Critically assess whether each criterion appears:

- Measurable; will it enable a judgement to be made?
- Clearly stated?
- Clinically sound?
- Professionally acceptable?
- Relative to only one topic?
- Relative to the standard?
- Relevant to the domain which it is to measure?
- Achievable?
- Realistic?
- Valid?

It will not be possible at this stage to assess reliability without testing the criteria in relationship to the standard. Choose the criteria which appear to have the above requirements and make sure they are in the correct sequence and logical order. Arrange criteria into statements or questions according to the approach being used.

If there are more good criteria than required, put them in some order of priority and save those not required for another time or in case the ones that were chosen proved not to be valid.

If a large number of standards are produced it is wise to put them into a master list and randomly select a specific number when needed. It will be appreciated that a computer eases the work of recording and randomly selecting standards and criteria.

Validation

To validate the standards and criteria means to verify their authenticity. The choice of how this is done depends on the individual groups. Some groups test a number of standards as they progress; for example, every two standards are tested and then refined. We prefer to complete the project and put the standards into an instrument. However, it does depend on the number of standards that were set, the time taken and the confidence of the group members and what they feel is the most effective way for their area. The number of standards to go into an instrument may depend on the number of criteria to be evaluated.

Before testing the instrument and the individual standards and criteria, write a protocol (guidelines) for carrying out the test. Negotiate with the manager and senior nurse to test the instrument in an appropriate area and arrange a suitable date and time. The people carrying out the test should understand what is required. The people whose work will be evaluated will be told the purpose of the exercise, that it is to test the quality measuring instrument, the standards and the criteria. It is also sensible to carry out interobserver reliability testing.

'This is defined as the level of agreement between observers (auditors) meaning what percentage of time do two or more observers, collecting data from the same source and at the same time agree on what they have observed'.

(cited in Kemp, 1983)

'This is an attempt to ensure that the auditors perceive the criteria similarly thus aiding objective judgement. If the level of agreement is too low it may indicate that the instrument is not valid or reliable for a particular area. However, a word of caution; it may mean the auditors do not fully understand what is required and have been poorly prepared. Any failings should be corrected before the test begins.

Patients' permission must be sought before they are asked questions that relate to the test.

Having tested the instrument, listen to the views of the auditors. Discuss the scores with those whose work was evaluated. Closely examine the findings. We have already made some comments about interobserver reliability, but also check if the written questions which the auditor had to ask were phrased in an objective manner, so the patient or staff member's response could not be manipulated. Also examine the instructions given to the auditors. Were they clearly stated so that they could carry out their work correctly?

When examining the instrument check that the layout is easy to use. Were the criteria in sequence. Look again at the protocol and consider if the environment was right for the auditing to be carried out. Did the criteria focus on the right patient group?

Examine the scores. Were all the criteria evaluated and if not, why not? Be as vigilant in reviewing high scores as low scores. Do the criteria have all the necessary attributes of a criterion? Were all the resources available to enable the standard to be met?

Examine the standard. Is it written in the right tense? Does it, too, have all the required characteristics? It must be remembered that if a standard is altered then the criteria must also be reviewed.

Having reviewed the test findings, the standard setting group members should develop a plan to overcome the deficiencies. There may be a need to discard some of the standards and criteria. This may be stressful but it will be cost effective in the long run. When the deficiencies have been corrected, retest the instrument and any standards or criteria which have been altered. Once the standards are found to be valid and reliable they should be given to the appropriate body to be ratified.

It is appropriate here to refer once more to measurement which is not an easy concept to describe. Plutchik (1968) defines it as:

> The assignment of numbers to objects or events according to certain rules. It appears there are at least two good reasons for doing this. One is that numbers represent a universal language for describing many different kinds of things; the other is that numbers enable us to make finer magnitude distinction than would otherwise be possible.

We have proposed an instrument that requires a yes or no response to which will be assigned a numerical value which enables people to discriminate between good and poor care by having a score or index of the quality of that care.

An area of debate is whether criteria should be assigned different weights, according to the importance of the criteria. The weighting will not only require statistical skills, but also at times philosophical and ethical debate and decisions. It seems to us that, at this stage in the development of quality measuring instruments for patients' nursing care, equal weight should be given to all criteria. There is a need for further research in this area.

An instrument which calls for a yes or no response is easier to handle than one that calls for judgement such as poor care, average care, good care. We believe such judgement to be too subjective. However, instruments that do use such evaluation techniques usually assign a score to their judgements.

The procedure for obtaining a percentage score is as follows:

1. 'Yes' is scored 1.
2. 'No' is scored 0.
3. Deduct the number of 'not applicable' responses (if that facility is available) from the total number of questions or observations which could have been scored. This gives the number of applicable responses.
4. From the number of applicable responses identify and add the number of 'yes' scores.
5. Divide the number of 'Yes' responses by the total of applicable responses and multiply by 100 to obtain a percentage score.

For example:

25 questions
5 not applicable
20 applicable responses
14 'Yes' responses
$14 \div 20 = 0.7 \times 100 = 70$ per cent quality score or index.

All quality results must be reviewed, including any 'not applicables', to identify the need for corrective action or praise.

A decision has to be made about the level of quality required. It is not sufficient to use such terms as *minimum (safe) standards, acceptable standards* or *optimum standards*. A numerical score has to be assigned to the terms which denote levels of quality. For example, optimum level ('most favourable condition', *Concise Oxford Dictionary* 1982) may be 100 per cent. Acceptable level may be 80 per cent. Minimum or safe care maybe 50 per cent.

Ideally all standard setting groups should have access to someone with statistical skills to help them with measurement but as this is not likely to be available to most groups, keep the measurement simple.

Having discussed a number of aspects that relate to standard setting we now move to our final chapter in which we focus on audit. This is in part about using standards.

References

Barnett, D.E. and Kemp, N. (1994) *The A to Z Reference of Applied Quality for Clinical Managers in Hospitals*. Chapman and Hall, London (in press).

Benner, P. (1984) *From Novice to Expert: Excellence and Power in Clinical Nursing Practice*. Addison – Wesley, California.

Department of Health (1991) *The Patient's Charter*. HMSO, London.

Donabedian, A. (1966) Evaluating the quality of medical care. *Millbank Memorial Fund Quarterly*, **44**, 166–203.

Garvey, A. and Manley, K. (1992) Understanding quality. RCN Nursing Update. *Nursing Standard*, **16**, 3–8.

Concise Oxford Dictionary (1982) Sykes, J.B.(ed.). Oxford University Press, Oxford.

Kemp, N. (1983) *Quality Assurance Programmes and the Nursing Process*. Florence Nightingale/Smith & Nephew Scholarship Report. The Florence Nightingale Committee, London.

Kemp, N. (1985) *Patient's Views of Quality Care for Surgical Nursing. Patients' Survey*. Unpublished work.

Kemp, N. and Richardson, E. (1990) *Quality Assurance in Nursing Practice*. Butterworth Heinemann, London.

Kitson, A. (1988) *Nursing Quality Assurance, Dynamic Standard Setting System*. RCN, London.

Mason, E.J. (1984) *How to Write Meaningful Standards*, 2nd edn. John Wiley, New York.

Maxwell, R.J. (1984) Perspectives in NHS management. Quality assessment in health. *British Medical Journal*, **288**, 1470–2.

Miles,M. (1993) Personal communication.

Miles M., Homer P. (1993) West Dorset Community Health NHS Trust. Care Standards, Quality Dimension. *Effectiveness* (Practice). Unpublished.

Plutchik, R. (1968) *Foundations of Experimental Research*. Harpers Experimental Psychology Series. Harper and Row, London.

Price Waterhouse. (1987) *Excelcare – Nursing Management Information System*. Price Waterhouse, Bristol.

Reid, W.K. (1992) *Health Service Commission for England, for Scotland and for Wales Annual Report for 1992*. HMSO, London.

Royal College of Nursing (1979) *Standards of Nursing Care*. RCN, London.

Royal College of Nursing (1981) *Towards Standards*. RCN, London.

Royal College of Nursing (1986) *Standards of Care Project. Check List on How to Write Standards of Nursing Care*. RCN, London.

Royal College of Nursing (1990) *Quality Patient Care. The Dynamic Standard Setting System*. RCN, London.

Tingle, J. (1992) Legal implications of standard setting in nursing. *British Journal of Nursing*, **1**, 728–31.

United Kingdom Central Council (1992) *Code of Professional Conduct*. UKCC, London.

World Health Organisation (1981) *Health Programme Evaluation*. WHO, Geneva.

Zimmer, M.J. (1974) Guidelines for the development of outcome criteria. *Nursing Clinics of North America*, **9**, 2317–21.

11

Auditing the quality of care

In this book we have tried to emphasise the importance of the individual and the need to ensure that all aspects of care are planned and given in a way which assures quality of care. We have considered the ways in which nurses attempt to set standards for the work they do and, bearing in mind that we are now in a market economy we have looked at the effects of a cost-conscious, value for money ethic on the quality of nurses' work.

In this last chapter we will discuss the concept of audit as it applies to health care but in particular how it affects nurses, and, most importantly, how it can improve the quality of care for the individual. Practitioners are now concerned not just to state a range of quality measures but also to use these measures to indicate where action needs to be taken when standards are not being met. There has always been within the nursing process a stage when an evaluation of the outcome of care has been considered. As stated earlier this could be considered as part of the audit procedure; 'The philosophy behind nursing audit is that nurses are accountable for the care they give, and this must be of good quality' (Toms, 1992).

The word *audit* is thought of most often in terms of accounting and the work of auditors as that of checking accounts; the *Concise Oxford Dictionary* (1991) refers to audit as 'an official examination of accounts'. Salvage cited by Malby (1991) describes audit as 'a word used to indicate a cycle of activity, to look at what you are currently doing, determine what you should be doing and take action to close the gap between the real and the ideal". That cycle of activity is generally thought to contain a number of items Malby (1992) states that 'This cycle involves systematic review of practice, identification of problems, development of possible solutions, implementation of change, and then further review'. Stewart and Craig, cited by Toms (1992), relate audit to care by describing it as 'a systematic method of obtaining, appraising, and reporting information about facets of care'.

This notion of a cycle is well illustrated in the NHS Management Executive's Teaching Notes on Nursing Audit as shown in Figure 11.1.

1. The cycle begins with the observation of practice; in particular the nurse describes an aspect of practice and the standards of care which she is using in carrying out that practice.
2. Discussions must then take place between colleagues in order to agree what is good practice and thus to set standards.
3. Comparisons can now be made between the newly determined standards and current practice by collecting relevant data.
4. This will then allow for the monitoring of the quality of care at whatever level the standards have been checked.
5. If standards are not being met then it will be necessary to develop an action plan in order to determine ways of improving the situation. This needs to be agreed with colleagues who may be involved.
6. When this action plan has been put into practice it will then be necessary to monitor the changes which have occurred, observing the effects and hopefully noting the improvements which have taken place.

'If this is used with conviction then it will result in a systematic improvement of nursing practice'. (NHS Management Executive, 1991).

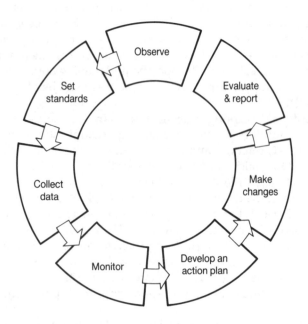

Fig. 11.1.   The process of audit

There are a number of approaches to audit and to its cycle as described above. Primarily these are dependent on the health care professionals' philosophy of quality and on its implementation within the organisation. Where total quality management is in operation it is likely that a system will be set up to systematically assess all identified aspects of performance against standards. This will occur at all levels within the organisation and consider all elements of the delivery of health care. Audit scores thus obtained can be used to identify the strengths and weaknesses related to practice within that organisation and thus allow action to be agreed to improve practice.

An alternative approach is that of quality improvement, which focuses on defined areas of health care. This is generally carried out by a group of multidisciplinary professionals whose concern the area is. However, the group must be aware that in improving one area of care they may affect other areas, even to the extent of putting an added strain on the resources of that area.

On a recent visit to Washington one of the authors was interested to see this approach used on an obstetric unit. Due to the high cost of inpatient care it is the custom in the hospital concerned for newly delivered mothers to spend one night only as an inpatient. This means that any time available for health education of these mothers, who incidentally come on the whole from a disadvantaged background as far as health care is concerned, is strictly limited. The nurses on this unit decided that an area requiring quality improvement was the education of mothers in the feeding of their babies. This was then targeted on all care plans to ensure that this above all was included in the patient's care.

Although nurses in this country have been writing standards of care for several years they have not unfortunately always used them as a measure of the quality of the care being given. Many nurses asked about standards of care, know them as a file in sister's office or as the outcome of a working group's activities but not always as a means of measuring the quality of patient care. However, nursing audit is not new; in the 1960s in the USA, Phaneuf (1976) had already developed a nursing audit tool which is still in use today. This tool is a 50 item scale designed to measure retrospectively the quality of care received by a patient during a particular cycle of care. The audit is carried out by an audit committee of nurses who meet monthly to examine aspects of care as recorded in nursing records. This in itself may have limited application but it does reflect on how well the record is written. It is always worth remembering that in litigation it is the records which are examined first.

The 1980s in Britain saw the development of Monitor (Goldstone *et al.*), the anglicised version of Rush Medicus Quality Monitoring Methodology and other similar tools such as the Quality Assurance Tool of the National Association of Theatre Nurses. These tools both use a variety of methods of obtaining data. Nursing records are also used, but the assessors in both cases also observe practice and ask questions of both nurses and patients.

At this time, however, audit in health care had a fairly low profile. The major catalyst for raising this profile has been the government's White Paper *Working for Patients* published in 1989. In particular this alerted the medical profession to their responsibility in this area, a responsibility which had been identified the previous year by the Royal College of Physicians' publication *Medical Audit; A First Report. What, Why, and How?* This report suggested that all medical practitioners should be auditing their sphere of working practice.

The White Paper *Working for patients* stated quite clearly that doctors were to engage in 'systematic, critical analysis of the quality of medical care, including the use of resources and the resulting outcome and quality of life for patients'. There is general acknowledgement 'that the central purpose of medical audit is to improve practice' (Harman and Martin, 1992). It has a number of definitions. It may be described as a retrospective review and evaluation of medical records which is carried out to assess the care which has been provided. Clearly the White Paper's description suggests something rather more comprehensive than this. June Huntington (1990) states that, 'Medical audit is best described as a required educational activity in the context of a managed service'. However, it must always be acknowledged that the improvement of identified deficiencies and their subsequent correction is its prime purpose.

Since the concept was introduced in this country the *British Medical Journal* has consistently reported developments in all aspects of medical audit. In September 1990 a review of the experience of the introduction of medical audit into one of the North West Thames area hospitals was reported. The article by Gabbay *et al.* (1990) is interesting as it discusses the difficulties faced in introducing a new activity into the lives of already very busy professionals. There was clear recognition of the inevitability of the process and perhaps the advantages of being in the vanguard of an innovative activity. In retrospect the authors admitted that they met with far less resistance to its introduction than they had imagined.

An initial pilot scheme for this project provided 'appreciable improvements in aspects of care such as clerking and record keeping'. It also initiated the writing of agreed standards that allow more objective measurement. The analysis of the audit of clinical mangement has resulted in the development of explicit guidelines which are now being further developed.

Those participating in this initial work also observe that 'the classic elegance of the audit cycle is far more muddled in the real world'

(Gabbay *et al.* 1990). The very fact of observing practice caused the standards of that practice to improve. Revised audit documents improved the range of information available. One practical result of this was the obvious duplication that exists between the medical and nursing assessment and thus the need for greater sharing and cooperation in recording patient information.

One lesson arising from an examination of this early work was the amount of administration and organisation which it involved. This was one of the early concerns echoed by Huntington (1990) when she stated that 'an effective audit system will claim huge resources'. As with the implementation of any major change the initial introduction of audit does need to be well managed. Professional staff, not only medical practitioners, already have demanding schedules of work and some of the administrative elements of the audit process have inevitably been assigned to other individuals. This has often meant the employment of a new work force. Although the numbers in individual establishments may not be high, when this is multiplied throughout the country it is significant. It is therefore essential that the results of audit are seen to be not only cost-effective but also very clearly raising the standards of care for individuals. It would also be particularly helpful if the experience of audits could be shared, thus reducing some repetition of work.

An article in the BMJ in September 1991 by Firth-Cozens and Venning describe the advent of the audit officer in her many guises.The range of titles and the backgrounds of these individuals seem to vary enormously. Most people would seem to agree that a background in the NHS is at least helpful in understanding the organisation and that an interest and some experience in data collection and analysis is more helpful than specific professional orientation. There is no doubt that as audit is here to stay, so is this new group of staff. The provision by the King's Fund of a network newsletter for medical audit professionals undoubtedly supports their existence.

The introduction of medical audit became a requirement in all hospitals performing NHS work by April 1991.The effective implementation of this work has caused a number of concerns not least as it affects the differing perspectives of clinicians and managers. A paper discussing the possible divergence of views on this subject by these two groups appeared in the *Journal of the Royal College of Physicians of London* in April 1992. In their article, Smith *et al.* (1992) indicate that while managers and clinicians agree 'about the potential benefits of audit they had divergent opinions regarding its disadvantages'. Their work was based on a survey conducted in the North Staffordshire health district of health service managers and clinical consultants. Clinicians were primarily concerned that 'audit would interfere with clinical activity and divert resources that would be better used for patient care'. Managers did not fully share these concerns as they had hopes that audit would improve efficiency. The other major difference was in the concept of the time needed to conduct audit with the clinicians clearly expecting to spend more time than managers anticipated. The view is expressed that a recognition of differing perspectives is necessary but that their presence is not necessarily detrimental in itself.

This concern for the cost-effectiveness of extensive data gathering during the process of audit was raised by Balogh *ret al*. (1992). Certainly there is a need to be discriminating in the amount of audit information which may be gathered and not acted upon. 'The act of conducting audit serves as a catalyst by prompting people to reflect upon various aspects of their practice'.

In conducting nursing audit the same principles are used as in medical audit. The same reviews of health care which influenced medicine have also had an impact on nursing. Specifically the initiative led by the Chief Nurse at the Department of Health which produced the document *A Strategy for Nursing* (DHSS, 1986) included amongst its targets:

> There should be agreed policies and procedures for setting standards of care and monitoring their outcome; practitioners should develop a knowledge of quality assessment.

In 1993 our present Chief Nurse includes in *A Vision for the Future* (NHS Management Executive, 1993) a more up-to-date view of quality and the audit of nursing care:

> There is general consensus in the professions that providing patient care on an individual basis and developing and establishing monitoring and auditing systems in each provider unit and in primary health care are the foundation stones of a high quality service'.

However, it is clear that many nurses themselves are uncertain as to the meaning of nursing audit and the activities which it includes. A survey undertaken in Wales by Girvin (1992) revealed that there was 'considerable confusion over the terminology and the activities that could constitute audit'. All units approached were using educational audit but there was a wide variety of other activity including the use of 'off-the-shelf' tools such as Monitor. Some nurses thought that audit included examining such things as skill-mix, management and possibly personnel. The assessment of quality was sometimes only mentioned after prompting.

A smaller but similar review was carried out in the West Dorset General Hospitals Trust (Dodds and Ferguson, 1993). In response to a questionnaire 71 per cent of the nurses who replied did not know what was meant by nursing audit. As a result of this response a basic information booklet was produced and distributed to each ward. This included a number of definitions of nursing audit. One of those describes the fundamental principle behind audit as, 'to improve the quality of care delivered to the patient'. This is enhanced in the NHS Management Executive's definition in *Measuring the Quality* (1990) which states:

It is a system which allows nurses to measure their performance, recognise good practice and, if necessary, make improvements. It is developed with the help of colleagues and the support of management and it is an essential part of the general effort to deliver high quality care in all parts of the Health Service.

Most nurses base their understanding of nursing audit naturally on their own experience. In its response to the White Paper *Working for Patients*, Project 32 was set up by the NHS Management Executive to consider the variety of definitions of nursing audit and to address how this may be progressed. It has been very careful in its attempts to do so and suggests first that the term 'audit for nursing services' be used. This is described as incorporating:

. . . the systematic and critical analyses by nurses, midwives and health visitors, in conjunction with other staff, of the planning, delivery and evaluation of nursing and midwifery care, in terms of their use of resources and the outcomes for patients/clients and introduces appropriate change in response to that analysis'.

Nursing care audit is then seen as part of this more widely embracing audit.

When considering audit, nurses may first ask themselves what should be audited. Anything which can be measured in terms of professional, managerial or organisational aspects of nursing can be audited, and certainly anything which directly affects patient care could be included.

In Chapter 10 we used an example of a standard relating to Sleep: Noise and Disturbances at Night. This undoubtedly very much affects the quality of care a patient may receive and so the nurses of Selly Oak Hospital set out to audit this standard amongst others. From the audit protocol on page 116, you will see that their objective was 'To find out whether a suitably quiet environment is provided at night to facilitate sleep and rest'.

The results of that audit are summarised on page 118. This indicates clearly where action or otherwise is needed. The 100 per cent compliance for S2(c) is excellent. Activity S2(b) which relates to equipment has 80 per cent compliance which is also good but there are actions identified which, if taken, could increase the score still further.

It was indicated in an earlier chapter that cost of care has become an important issue and clearly when resources are being consumed then an audit tool should take account of these. The preparation for audit must

Audit Protocol

Audit objective: To find out whether a suitably quiet environment is provided at night to facilitate sleep and rest.
Time frame: One night a week for five weeks.
Sample: Five patients of varying ages and sex in different parts of the ward. . Total = 25.
Auditors:
Date:

Target group	Method	Code	Audit criteria
Patients	Ask	P1	Was nursing care to other patients carried out quietly?
		P2	Did patient receive an explanation prior to settling about any planned disturbance to their sleep?
		P3	Did patient receive an explanation about any unforseen disturbance in their sleep?
		P5	When speaking to each other, did nurses talk quietly?
Nurses	Observe	P6	Are all the nursing staff wearing quiet shoes on the night of the audit?
Ward Environment	Observe	S2	Are the following fixtures and fittings working quietly?
		a	all doors?
		b	ward trolleys?
		c	other ward furniture, e.g. commodes, drip stands, etc.
		P7	Between 2300 hours and 0630 hours are all:
		a	telephones on quiet ringing tone?
		b	call bells on night level?
		c	lights on dim?
		P8	Is the ward 'quiet' notice in place from 2300 to 0700 hours?

be carefully considered and this will include the choice and preparation of the auditors.

Conducting the audit itself has financial implications and these must be considered. Costs will include staff time for the creation of the audit tool, if a local tool is to be designed, for its implementation and for its subsequent review. Results of the audit have to be processed. Time and resources must be set aside for those and for any action which may be necessary as a result of the findings. In any such undertaking information systems are necessary to allow others to fully appreciate the significance of the audit and their individual roles within the system.. However any costs incurred must be set against the potential savings from an improved service and better patient care. Consumers will certainly benefit from any quality improvement, thus raising their confidence in an efficient and effective service. Clearly priorities must be established and any resulting benefits identified before making a final decision regarding the audit mechanism.

It is our contention that whenever an innovation such as auditing is introduced there are two management considerations which must be given priority if the scheme is to be in any way successful. These are communication and education. All staff need to know what it involves for them personally and where their role is in relation to its implementation. Some will clearly be more involved than others. This may be in terms of their management responsibilities or because they perhaps have been part of an earlier standard setting group. The timing of information in relation to the implementation is also important. Too early and it will be forgotten, too late and it will not have the impact intended and, worse, perhaps serve to create anxiety and resistance.

Decisions also have to be made as to whether the auditors will be local members of staff or whether they will be brought in from outside and thus, in theory, be more objective. The latter may also be prepared specifically for their role and thus may not be distracted by other concerns while auditing in clinical areas. However, they may well miss the nuances which only members of staff may be sensitive to.In order to ensure that the care of individual patients is of good quality it is vital that those measuring care know what they are looking at and how the tool they have been given should accurately be used. Some clinical areas identify a member of staff to take on the role of audit nurse. She should then be specifically prepared for her role, so that she is aware not just of the mechanism of the audit tool but also her responsibilities in relation to the scores she obtains and the feedback which is given to staff as a result.

It is not only the score which is important but also its implication for the quality of the care delivered, both at the level of the individual practitioner and for her patient.There may be consequences also in relation

Audit Summary

Audit objective:	To find out whether a suitably quiet environment is provided at night to facilitate sleep and rest.
Time frame:	One night per week for five weeks.
Sample:	25 patients.
Auditors:	
Date:	13 February 1992 – 26 March 1992.
Reference:	ASUM0017.
Hospital	Selly Oak Hospital, Medical Ward.

Activity	Findings	Conclusions
P1 and P5 How quietly did nurses talk and perform their duties after lights out?	80% and 80% compliance. Patients very complimentary on the effort by nurses to carry out their duties quietly	Very busy night in week three/four. Patients in *first two bays* more disturbed in week four.
P3 Explanation given to patients on planned disturbance.	78% compliance. *No explanation* about moving beds. Explanation for other disturbances *very good.*	Patients appeared to accept the disturbances of admissions, *after explanation*. More critical of disturbance caused by *confused patients*, even after explanation.
P2 Did patient have planned disturbances explained?	70% compliance. Patients very au fait with necessary routine disturbances – drugs, obs., etc.	70% compliance excellent result, in view of some very busy nights during the survey.
S2 (b) Oxygen cylinders.	Moved around on numerous occasions. No buffers to stop cylinder banging against metal holder. 80% compliance.	Rubber buffers required on oxygen stands at bottom of cylinder and half way up.
Kitchen machinery	*Noisy,* particularly on quiet nights	Doors need to be kept closed when working in the kitchen.
S2 (c) Ward lights	100% compliance. Every effort had been made to reduce unnecessary light. Every effort had also been made to give patients maximum rest by delaying switching on main ward lights each morning.	A very welcome result for patients who were convalescing.

to the medical practitioner who may be intent on buying care for his patients from the Trust in which the nurse operates.

Nurses sometimes feel that audit has a certain mystique attached to it and that only specially prepared individuals or those employed for the purpose should participate, but audit is the prerogative of all nurses as all nurses have a responsibility to ensure that standards are upheld and that resources are used wisely. In practical terms some nurses will be more directly involved than others. This may depend on the method which any organisation may choose and the level within the organisation at which the individual nurse operates. Each nurse who has responsibility for the care planned and delivered to individual patients should be able to measure and correct any deficiencies in the care thus provided.

How is nursing audit carried out? First, this process of measuring and recording should be seen in the context of the other activities of the quality assurance cycle. This cycle has four stages as described in *Framework of Audit for Nursing Services* (NHS Management Executive, 1991b). These are:

1. **Objective/standard setting**. It is necessary to define what is to be achieved for the area of care the audit will cover. This should contain standards to indicate the quality measures.
2. **Implementation**. This means putting into practice policies and procedures which have been agreed and carrying out care as prescribed. The prescription of care should be based on the standards set.
3. **Measuring and recording**. This stage is the one which most people would recognise as the audit process. Here the nurse is using some predetermined means of measuring data in a systematic and objective way.

   Some of these means were mentioned earlier with reference to 'off-the-shelf' tools. They can include examining records, observing nursing actions, asking questions of both staff and patients. It should also be remembered that there are situations where it is more appropriate to ask one level of staff than another, for example, students rather than qualified staff. It may also be necessary to question not just patients themselves but also their friends and relatives. There is also the question of the patient who cannot speak for himself and whether the nurse as his advocate or the relative or friend is the more appropriate source of information.

   As audit is concerned to achieve change in practice as a result of an identified deficit in care, it is necessary to use as precise a measuring tool as possible. The precision of the tool does not necessarily lie in its complexity. The most important element perhaps is to ensure that the data collected are useful and can actually be used in the way specified.

4. **Monitoring and action plan**. The information collected must be used to make changes where these are found necessary. These changes may affect policies and procedures but they may also lead to a revision of the standards themselves. It must always be remembered that the first attempt at setting standards is rarely likely to be the definitive one, no matter the time and trouble taken to write them.

As stated earlier there have been initiatives in auditing nursing practice for many years in this country. One of those well documented in the *Nursing Times* was the Doncaster Management Audit which was published in 1973. This audit was associated with the roles and responsibilities of nurses initially in management positions in the service and was linked to staff appraisal. Amongst its identified advantages was that, 'It identifies weaknesses in good nursing care practices and aspects of the nursing service which need to be developed'. Although its recognised aim was to evaluate nursing management performance, the principles apply to all forms of nursing audit. Key factors of this process as identified by Huczynski (1980) are:

- the need to clarify one's objectives for introducing audit;
- gaining the commitment and support of the nurses who will be involved in it;
- establishing communication systems to provide adequate and regular feedback to staff;
- committing oneself to a programme of education for staff to help them;
- fully understanding the purpose of the audit scheme.

Sometimes the audit will take the form of a monitoring document. One of the authors designed such a tool (Kemp, 1978) in order to audit documents used in the nursing process. The following (page 121) is an example of some of the items in this document. There are a clear set of instructions for the use of the document and for the action to be taken at the end of the audit.

Another variation on this is the system which is used with the Excelcare programme. This system makes use of a unit of care evaluation form, an example of which is reproduced below. This refers to the standard relating to patient admission which is described on page 122.

	Yes	No	Comments

Evaluation

Is a statement written at
the time of review?

Is a new review date set?

Is the statement dated and
signed?

Do evaluation statements appear
explicit?

Are modifications made to the
care plan as a result of
the evaluation?

Is there evidence that the patient
was involved in the evaluation?

Is an action crossed through
when it ceases to be effective?

Is the new nursing prescription
to solve or modify the problem
written in the action column?

Is the goal crossed through if
no longer realistic?

Was the goal inappropriate – if
so, was a new goal set?

Is the problem crossed through
when it ceases to be a problem?

Review

Is this a realistic time to
review the patient's status
and care?

NB

Does the care plan indicate an
understanding of the concept of
individualised patient care?

(Kemp, 1978)

West Dorset Hospital patient evaluation form.

Date: 21/09/93   EXCELCARE (tm) Quality Assurance   Page: 1
Time: 12:58   WEST DORSET HOSPITAL
                          Patient Evaluation Form

Patient: Bed: B10   Review Date: 09/21/93

1006   N/F IN ADMISSION
1009   N/F IN MEDICAL PROCEDURES & INVESTIGATIONS

Were Standards Met?

YES	NO	Standards
		*** 1006 N/F IN ADMISSION 1. Please ask the patient if they are prepared to be interviewed by a nurse to answer a few questions to help monitor the quality of patient care. 1. Did the nurses make you feel comfortable and at ease on admission? 2. Did the nurses introduce themselves? 3. Can you name your Primary/Named nurse? 4. Did the nurses inform you of the following: A. The ward information booklet? B. The visiting hours? C. The catering arrangements? D. The toilet facilities?

Various initiatives are at present in place throughout the country; one such is described by Morison (1991) as the Stirling model of nursing audit. This was developed to build on the quality assurance initiatives which were already under way in the organisation. The aims of the project were:

• to improve the quality of patient care;
• to make the most efficient use of resources;
• to foster in nurses a critical questioning approach to their activities and the needs of their patients.

Morison underlines the need to be positive in the approach to the introduction of nursing audit as the concept often has a negative and critical feel to it amongst staff. The importance of education in the introduction of any change cannot be overstated. As part of this programme staff should be made to feel responsible for identifying the priorities for their own local audit projects. Emphasis must be on choosing items which can have the greatest impact on direct patient care and thus improve the quality of that care for the individual. In differing clinical specialities the emphasis may be different.

This need for education and the impact of change resulting from the introduction of audit is acknowledged by Malby (1992). However, she takes the argument a stage further. It is not enough merely to establish ways of conducting nursing audit and as a result having available a measurable review of current practice, but, when the need for change is identified, the means to support and effect the necessary change must also be readily available to nurses.

Malby clearly advocates the need for a strategy for change. The need to recognise the interests of all those affected by the results of audit must be acknowledged within this strategy. These may be complex and even conflicting. It is anticipated that as a result of audit nursing developments will occur which will enhance the quality of care but these may only take place if the organisation itself has given sufficient thought and commitment to their implementation. Malby concludes her article with the following telling statement:

> The organisation's commitment to supporting effective nursing audit will need to commence with the development of change agent posts to lead nursing developments, along with effective education programmes for the post holders to develop the key skills required to lead change.

This clearly has important implications for nurse managers if we believe this is necessary.

When nursing audit is set up as part of a nursing quality assurance programme, it is important that the purpose of the audit is clearly identified. In West Dorset General Hospitals Trust the Excelcare nursing information system is used to assess and plan nursing care. The system also facilitates the development of nursing audit as the information it provides includes incidence of nursing problems, their related interventions and nursing outcomes. A project funded by the Wessex Regional Health Authority's research and development directorate aimed to raise the level of understanding and awareness of the importance of quality assurance by highlighting the role of nursing audit within the trust. In order to achieve this it was necessary to identify training needs before introducing the Excelcare quality monitoring tool across the Trust. This resulted in the production and distribution of necessary information.

When setting up an audit, nurses should first be very clear about the aspect of care they are choosing, e.g. in West Dorset one aspect of care chosen was the presence of pressure sores. Identifying such topics may in itself take some considerable time to achieve. Having done so it will then be necessary to agree the level of acceptability, in this case, for the presence of pressure sores. This may be identified using local knowledge or by doing a literature search and accepting an identified percentage from work done on a wider, perhaps national scale. It may then be necessary to identify any exceptions which are justified for clinically valid reasons. In this instance, nurses may agree that there could be no allowed exceptions. It would finally be necessary for nurses to determine what constitutes a pressure sore, how it would be recognised or measured and in what time frame the presence of the pressure sore would be identified. This detail is sometimes described as setting the audit protocol. You will recall that this term was used by the nurses whose audit criteria were considered in relation to sleep.

Once this system is set up then it is important to decide how often the audit is carried out. There are many factors which have to be considered in making this decision, some of which are necessarily organisational and dependent on resources available, particularly in relation to time including that necessary to take action on the result and to give the necessary feedback. It may be necessary to write a specific action plan and consider the need for producing guidelines for good practice at this stage, hence improving quality. The extent and scope of the audit also are important factors as is the priority of the information required. Audit tools mentioned earlier in the chapter each have different time scales for their operation. These may vary from once to three times in any one year. The repetition of the audit process may also depend on the score obtained at the previous audit. Where there are areas of concern it will be necessary to repeat the audit process at more frequent intervals than originally intended.

In considering audit nurses should also be aware of other audit processes which will influence their practice. In areas used for the clinical experience of student nurses the clinical learning environment audit has been in use for several years. This in particular examines the fitness of such areas to support the learning and developing competence of the student nurse at various stages of her course. This audit should examine the following areas:

- the ethos of the placement;
- organisation of care
- supervision and mentorship
- teaching programme and assessment
- research basis of care planning and delivery
- academic and professional qualifications of clinical staff

- staff development programme
- physical environment.

(English National Board, 1993)

It will be immediately obvious that several of these sections are likely to be considered in an audit concerned with direct patient care and may already be examined within other documentation.

The English National Board is also concerned to widen the scope of educational audit to all areas educational activity for which it has responsibility. To quote from their document *Guidelines for Educational Audit* (ENB, 1993): 'Quality in education is a journey, not a destination, and the search for quality must be a continuous, systematic process which exists in institutions that have a desire to improve and develop'.

Organisational audit is also familiar to some nurses. This is an approach to auditing which is based on the accreditation systems in operation in the United States, Canada, Australia and New Zealand. The system in this country was developed by the King's Fund in 1989. It is designed to cover the wide range of services which an acute hospital has to offer.

> Organisational audit offers a framework of standards that facilitates the systematic review of hospital organisation and the systems and processes that should be in place in order to provide an efficient and effective service.

(Pitt, 1990a)

The principles of auditing as described above apply in this situation but clearly the scale is larger and the audit itself is carried out by a team of senior health care professionals who have been prepared by the King's Fund for their task.

This last variation of the audit process does bring together all aspects of the organisation concerned with the care of patients and surely it is to the benefit of patients to have these considered collectively. The Royal College of Nursing in its formal evidence on the government's White Paper to the Social Services Select Committee stressed that to be effective, 'The audit process must be multidisciplinary'. The accepted terminology for this combined approach is *Clinical audit*. The multidisciplinary approach which this implies 'is much more likely to produce an assessment of patient outcome which matches the patient's own perception than medical audit alone' (Hancock, 1990).

The effect of this combined approach to the quality of care is illustrated by Carruthers and Bennett (1991) in relation to the patient who has had a hip replacement.

> The proportion of patients able to return to an active life after a total hip replacement depends not just on the quality of the surgical process, but on the quality of all components of the whole clinical episode'.

In this, it is not just doctors and nurses who are concerned but also the paramedical, the laboratory staff and many others providing an array of support services.

In an earlier chapter we discussed the use of collaborative care plans. One region in this country has taken this concept a stage further and produced a form of collaborative auditing (Carlisle, 1991). This grew out of a trip made to the USA by a group of health care staff to examine a model for clinical auditing in the UK. The result was a joint effort in bringing together all the people involved in care planning and ensuring that what was planned for the patient was all part of the same documentation.

> This sort of care planning can produce prospective clinical audit, in which patients' care is planned, evaluated and changed while they are in hospital. All disciplines are involved in this process.
>
> (Finnegan, 1991)

Patients also manage better if they are better informed about their care and subsequent health needs. The quality of all aspects of communication is vital and can only work well where there is collaboration between all health care professionals in the pursuance of quality. The cycle of audit is complete when policies are changed in response to the need to improve practice in areas where weaknesses have been identified.

With commitment to examine care in this way and to do something about the results which allows the improvement in care then each individual patient cannot help but benefit.

References

Balogh, R., Parker, K. (1992) Off the shelf audit: is it feasible? *Nursing Standard*, **7**(1), 35–8.

Carlisle, D. (1991) Collaborative auditing. *Nursing Times*, **87**(2), 30–1.

Carruthers, I. and Bennett, S. (1991). Better audit, better health. *Health Service Journal*, **101**(5282), 28–9.

Concise Oxford Dictionary. 1991. Allen R (ed). Oxford University Press, Oxford.

Department of Health (1989) *Working for Patients*. HMSO, London.

Department of Health & Social Security Nursing Division (1986) *Strategy for Nursing*. HMSO, London.

Dodds, F. and Ferguson, S. (1993) *Excelcare: Quality Assurance and Nursing Audit Project: Second Report*. West Dorset General Hospitals NHS Trust, unpublished report.

English National Board (1993) *Guidelines for Educational Audit*. ENB, London.

Finnegan, E. (1991). Collaborative auditing. *Nursing Times*, **87**(2), 30–1.

Firth-Cozens, J. and Venning, P. (1991) Audit officers: what are they up to? *British Medical Journal*, **303**, 631–2.

Gabbay, J., McNicol M., Spiby, J. (1990) What did audit achieve? Lessons from preliminary evaluation of a year's medical audit. *British Medical Journal*, **301**, 526–9.

Girvin, J. (1992) Understanding nursing audit. *Nursing Times*, **88**(29), 58–9.

Goldstone, L.A., Ball, J.A., Collier, M.M. (1984). *Monitor – An Index of the Quality of Nursing Care for Acute Surgical and Medical Wards*. Unique Business Services Ltd, University of Northumbria at Newcastle-upon-Tyne.

Hancock, C. (1990) 'Can it work for patients?' *Senior Nurse*, **10**(7), 8–10.

Harman, D. and Martin, G. (1992) *Managers and medical audit*. Health Services Management, April, 27–9.

Huczynski, A.A. (1980) Practical issues in the implementation of nursing management audit. Occcasional Papers, *Nursing Times*, **76**(4), 13–16.

Huntington, J. (1990) In the pursuit of good quality. *The Health Service Journal*, **100**, 521.

Kemp, N. (1978) *Monitoring the Nursing Process*. Unpublished.

Malby, R. (1991) Audit ability. *Nursing Times*, **87**(19), 35–7.

Malby, R. (1992) The process of change in nursing audit. *British Journal of Nursing*, **1**(4), 205–7.

Morison, M.J. (1991) The Stirling model of nursing audit. *Professional Nurse*, **6**(7), 366, 368–70.

NHS Management Executive (1993) *A Vision for the Future*. Department of Health, London.

NHS Management Executive (1991a) *Measuring the Quality – Nursing Care Audit*. Department of Health Nursing Division, crown copyright, London.

NHS Management Executive (1991b) *Framework of Audit for Nursing Services*, Department of Health, London.

Nursing Times Occasional Papers. (1973) Management audit for the nursing services. *Nursing Times*, **69**, 411–13.

Phaneuf, M. (1976) *The Nursing Audit – Self Regulation in Nursing Practice*, 2nd edn. Appleton-Century-Croft, New York.

Pitt, C. (1990) Organisational audit: a national approach to setting and monitoring organisational standards. *International Journal of Health Care*, **33**), 13–16.

Royal College of Physicians (1989) *Medical audit – A First Report: What, Why and How?* RCP, London.

Rush Medicus, Nursing Process Quality Monitoring Instrument. (1974). Public Health Service Control No. 1, NU-24299. United States Department of Health, Education and Welfare, Washington DC.

Smith H.E., Russel G.I., Frew, A.J., Daweb, P.T. (1992) Medical audit: the differing perspectives of managers and clinicians. *Journal of the Royal College of Physicians of London,* **26**(2), 177–80.

Toms, E.C. (1992) Evaluating the quality of patient care in district nursing. *Journal of Advanced Nursing,* **17**, 1489–95.

West Dorset General Hospital NHS Trust. (1993). *Excelcare Quality Assurance and Nursing Audit Project.* Secondment Report. Dodds F., Ferguson S. April. Unpublished report.

Index